"Getting older is for the courageo[us ...] with *Resilience*, Michele Howe has [...] to strength, bravery, and a deeper faith. This biblical and practical book will be your guide on the nightstand of your future."

—**Pam Farrel, international speaker,**
**best-selling author of over forty-eight books,**
**including *Men Are Like Waffles, Women Are Like Spaghetti*,**
**and *Discovering Hope in the Psalms:***
***A Creative Bible Study Experience***

"If you long to live for something that will outlast your life, read this book. Michele Howe reveals the secrets of how to embrace the aging process while being intentional about using our energy, resources, influence, and opportunities for God's glory. *Joyous Faith* is filled with practical ideas and encouraging spiritual wisdom for the last half of life."

—**Carol Kent, speaker and author of**
***He Holds My Hand: Experiencing God's Presence and Protection***

"When asked to read Michele Howe's *Joyous Faith: The Key to Aging with Resilience* my first thought was, 'Of course! Who doesn't need more joyous faith?' But then that subtitle hit me smack between the eyes. 'Wait. What? This is a book for aging women? Me?' Sometimes I forget I'm middle-aged! I thought for sure I'd have it all figured out by the time I hit my fifties, but I have so much more to learn. Michele shares from a place of personal experience, as she opens up the Bible to deliver spiritual-growth takeaways. Aging gracefully never looked so good."

—**Kathy Carlton Willis, God's Grin Gal, author and speaker**

"Through the stages of a woman's heart and life, Michele Howe is a companionable guide in matters of faith, identity, and an appreciation for this wonder-full here and now. With personal reflection and action steps, *Joyous Faith* inspires us to embrace life's second half with such grace and joy that a legacy is born."

—**PeggySue Wells, best-selling author of *The Slave across the Street*,**
***Homeless for the Holidays*, and *Chasing Sunrise***

# Joyous Faith

# MICHELE HOWE

# *Joyous Faith*

## The Key to Aging with Resilience

HENDRICKSON
PUBLISHERS

**Joyous Faith: The Key to Aging with Resilience**

© 2019 Michele Howe

Hendrickson Publishers Marketing, LLC
P. O. Box 3473
Peabody, Massachusetts 01961-3473
www.hendrickson.com

ISBN 978-1-68307-258-4

*Printed in the United States of America*

*First Printing — December 2019*

Library of Congress Control Number: 2019948213

To Deb

You are a treasure among friends.
I can always count on you for great conversation,
delicious food, and a godly perspective.
And you make me laugh.

"Let us rejoice and be glad and give him the glory!"
(Revelation 19:7)

 *Contents*

Acknowledgments                                              xi

Introduction                                                  1

1. Where Does Faith Come into the Picture?                    7
2. Trusting God with the Uncertainties of Life              12
3. Your Plan, God's Portion                                 17
4. When the Process Is Part of the Healing                  22
5. Keeping an Account of God's Faithfulness                 27
6. Finding Your Purpose                                     31
7. Limitations Do Not Define You                            36
8. Living This Day Regret Free                              41
9. Transforming Your Trials into Comfort for Others         46
10. Stretching Yourself to Outdo Others in Love             51
11. Enter in (All the Way in)                               56
12. Remaining Hopeful When Life Interrupts                  61
13. Adjusting Relational Expectations for Good              66
14. It's Always Something
    (and That's a Good Thing)                               71
15. God Gives Grace for Our Needs                           75
16. Learning to Want What God Wants                         80
17. What to Do When the Losses Add Up                       84

18. Choosing to Cling to God Instead                               89
19. Developing Your "Prayer Walk"
    (Literally or Figuratively)                                    94
20. Leaning into Jesus for the Strength You Need                   99
21. Joyous Laughter: A Key to Aging
    with Resilience                                                104
22. Embracing Forgiveness, Even When
    It Costs You                                                   108
23. Becoming an Instrument of Reconciliation                       113
24. Cultivating Contentment                                        117
25. Creating Beautiful Spaces in This Temporary Place              121
26. Losing All You Have Until All You
    Have Is Jesus                                                  126
27. Help! Help! Help!
    Thank You! Thank You! Thank You!                               131
28. The Golden Rule of Prayer                                      136
29. Bitter and Sweet Make One Flavor                               140
30. Leaving a Legacy That Outlasts You                             144

Sources for Quotations                                             149

# *Acknowledgments*

In every calendar year there are beginnings and endings, both personal and professional. For me, I have the privilege (for the eleventh time) to call myself a Hendrickson author. Who would ever have guessed that way back in 1999, when I held my first published book by Hendrickson, I would still be calling the Hendrickson team my publishing family? But God knew! With every year that passes (and every new book that is published), I grow increasingly more aware of how immensely blessed I am to be associated with such a talented and godly team of professionals. Thank you, my friend, Patricia Anders. As editorial director, you continue to simultaneously amaze and inspire me. I always value your editorial input (and you are so gracious presenting your recommendations for changes to me). You know what I'm trying to say even when I don't have the words I'm searching for at my fingertips. My deepest appreciation and thanks to you always. A special thank you to Dave Pietrantonio, the unsung hero behind the management of Hendrickson's book production for almost forty years! To Meg Rusick, Maggie Swofford, Phil Frank, and Tina Donohue: each of you is so uniquely gifted in what you do to create a winning book (each and every time). I marvel at how my sometimes clumsily typed out words are transformed into a beautiful finished product for readers to hold in their hands and treasure as I do. Often when I'm writing I am also praying

"Help Help! Help!" followed by "Thank you! Thank you! Thank you!" Many of those prayers of thanks are extended on behalf of all of you, and I am most humbly grateful for each of you.

I also want to express my kindest appreciation to Bob Hostetler, who represents me at the Steve Laube Agency. Thank you, Bob, for listening to my heart's desires and standing beside me as we work to create another resource worthy of him.

# Introduction

> But he said to me, "My grace is sufficient for you, for my
> power is made perfect in weakness." Therefore, I will boast
> all the more gladly about my weaknesses, so that Christ's
> power may rest on me. That is why, for Christ's sake, I delight
> in weaknesses, in insults, in hardships, in persecutions,
> in difficulties. For when I am weak, then I am strong.
>
> 2 Corinthians 12:9–10

When I sat down at my computer some eighteen months ago and began searching for just the right words to describe how hard aging can be once you reach fifty years and beyond, I came up with a myriad of descriptions and real-life examples to make my pitch to the Hendrickson publishing team. The more difficult challenge was narrowing down the character qualities for learning how to age well—and remain joyful, faithful, strong, and resilient. Aren't these the words we want to describe ourselves as we live out the entirety of our lives in a way that brings God glory?

I realized that living in the state of Michigan for my entire life (save the four years when we resided just over the state line in Ohio) qualified me as a hardy soul. Michiganders are well acquainted with the four seasons and their wildly fluctuating temperatures, colorfully diverse foliage, and hundreds

1

of lakes in every shape and size (we are the Great Lake State after all). But the winters here are, in a word, brutal. In the winter months, urgent weather advisories ding our cell phones seemingly several times a day. Change by the minute is almost a given. You never know what type of weather-related challenge you are going to wake up to or woken in the middle of the night. Wind. Snow. Ice. Freezing rain. Flooding. Repeat. Repeat. Repeat. We Michiganders are hardy souls by nature because we have to be.

The fact is, many of character qualities that I deem essential to living in the Midwest are the very same we need to hone as we grow older. Let me elaborate. Aging is just like a Michigan winter. You enjoy a smattering of mild days with a rare glimmer of sunshine and you think to yourself, "This isn't so bad. I can handle this." Then an ice storm hits. The power lines go down, and suddenly it's dark and cold and more than a little bit scary. You really don't know how long you'll have to endure living without power. Sure, we have generators, but they don't supply enough energy for the range of normal activities of everyday life, so we necessarily have to focus on the essentials.

After several days of hunkering down (and hoping and praying), the ice starts to melt as the temperatures rise degree by degree and the sun actually shines so you feel its warmth on your face for a few brief minutes. You feel a sudden boost of energetic confidence, enough to actually venture out again into the elements and all feels right in the world. But this euphoric feeling doesn't last long. Right after the sun disappears at five o'clock, you receive a frantic call from a friend whose tire hit an only-in-Michigan-sized pothole and her car veered off into a ditch, leaving her stranded. Can you come and help?

Your friend's unexpected emergency jolts you back to the harsh reality of these treacherous Michigan winters. A week or so passes uneventfully until the next snow storm hits and the weather conditions are so extreme that everything closes down. Businesses. Restaurants. Schools. Churches. Emergency vehicles only are allowed on the road—until further notice. Cancellations of this magnitude can make you feel so out of control and frustrated that you sense a silent scream emerging from deep within. You feel both vulnerable and powerless.

The next morning you rise and open the curtains to look outside, while mentally preparing to spend a good part of your morning shoveling and snow-blowing your walkways and driveway. But you sigh with relief to discover that the weather forecast was wrong and this northeaster mercifully passed you by this time around. You thank the good Lord for giving you a whole day to get out of the house and complete all the errands you've had to postpone because of inclement weather—before the next storm hits. Because you know it will.

Get the idea? Aging is so like the endurance race of living through a Michigan winter. We may be in the midst of a relatively calm, illness-dormant stage, and are thinking to ourselves, "I don't know what the fuss is all about. This aging business isn't so bad." Then, without warning, we find ourselves on the receiving end of a scary medical diagnosis, and our first reaction is anything but calm and steady as she goes. Somehow, we are instinctively wise enough to lean in further to the faithful arms of Christ and we endure the storm in our life, emerging a little weather-beaten perhaps but stronger for it. "But he said to me, 'My grace is sufficient for you, for my power is made perfect in weakness.'"

Or maybe your personal aging challenge doesn't have anything to do with a physical illness. Perhaps it is living longer than your closest family members and dearest friends. Loneliness is the struggle of your heart, and some days it feels as though no one understands how deeply these losses cut into you. While you know that God is always close by, you long for the arms of a real person to hold on to you to keep you steady and warm. "Therefore, I will boast all the more gladly about my weaknesses, so that Christ's power may rest on me."

Another common challenge of aging is the eventual loss of stamina and energy we once took for granted. Maybe you're lamenting that you don't have the strength to clean your own house, mow your lawn, or maintain the upkeep in your lifelong home. These are losses to be sure. But in the grand scheme of life, our neediness forces us to rely more and more upon God for our daily needs to accomplish daily deeds. It also reminds us that we were created to live interdependently, not independently from others. Aging is the perhaps the season of life when we recognize our weaknesses and need for inter-dependence for the first time. "That is why, for Christ's sake, I delight in weaknesses, in insults, in hardships, in persecu-tions, in difficulties."

Aging requires us to take a very different view of life and death and on how we decide we are going to live the final years of our lives, be they many or few. It is settling ourselves squarely on the enduring promises of God and not budging an inch when trials and troubles assault us. It is being certain that God will finish the great redemptive work in us that he started, and living in confidence that he is always with us. It believes that since Christ died on the cross to save us from death, he will also supply everything else we need to live. It is resting in the truth that none of us is strong enough without the supernatural flow of the Holy Spirit surging through us—and that's okay. "For when I am weak, then I am strong."

I hope that as you begin reading through *Joyous Faith: The Key to Aging with Resilience*, you will find great comfort in the truth that our sovereign God is working in you and through you to impact others for eternity. I pray that you will discover the power of Jesus living in you each and every day, no matter how strong or weak you may feel at this very minute. My dearest desire is that we all realize that aging is a God-ordained, beautiful season of life because it tests us, stretches us, and pushes us in ways we never expected—for our good and for God's glory.

# Chapter 1

## Where Does Faith Come into the Picture?

"If you do not stand firm in your faith,
you will not stand at all."
Isaiah 7:9

*Faith is not the presence of warm religious feelings.*
*It's the knowledge that you walk before the God who hears.*
Edward Welch

My husband, Jim, and I were on our way to the largest hospital in our city. It was snowing, windy, and an overall blustery kind of day that begged a person to stay put inside, safe and warm. On that rather treacherous drive in, neither of us felt safe or warm. Just a week earlier, Jim's physician told him that his biopsy revealed melanoma in situ (the melanoma part is bad, but the in situ part is good because it meant the cancer hadn't spread).

So there we were, traveling to the hospital for his procedure to remove the cancerous cells and the surrounding tissue. In and out. That's what the nurse said it would be for my hubby. To my mind, however, it was a whole lot more than that. The entire situation reminded me of a set of dominos placed carefully in a line on the floor. Once the first domino fell, the entire line toppled over. Receiving an unwanted diagnosis of any kind (or bad news of any sort) is unsettling, but it can grow out of proportion if we allow our fearful (that is, faithless) imaginations to take over.

I had done my own private bit of wrestling over Jim's diagnosis and kept repeating to myself that "God is the Blessed Controller" of all things. God knew the exact moment when the first cell went awry and began multiplying into cancer. God was far more than distantly aware of my husband's prognosis than we were, and he was near us. The more I rehearsed that truth and other Scriptures that supported it, the calmer and more peaceful I felt. Then again, it wasn't me who was diagnosed with melanoma. So I asked Jim what he was thinking and feeling.

He told me that it had taken him a few days to process the word *cancer*, and even after that, he felt unmoored and a bit shocked. The day before his scheduled surgery, Jim's colleagues gathered around him and prayed for him. One teacher sensed that Jim felt afraid and prayed that God would replace any fear with perfect peace. Jim later relayed that conversation to me. He believed his colleague's prayer was effective because he hadn't lost any sleep and honestly felt no anxiety. Still, Jim continued on, saying he was trying to define how faith entered into the equation. Was faith a set of warm, fuzzy emotions that sheltered us from bad news? Or was faith more of a quiet confidence in God's perfect plan and care for us that had nothing to do with emotion? One or the other? Or both?

After a few minutes of silence, Jim reported that the previous evening, he had leisurely read the newspaper and watched a program on television, while appreciating the fact that he was able to sleep in a little later than normal the following morning because of the procedure time. Jim remarked that he had thoroughly enjoyed the whole evening, because deep inside he knew God was in control. He was therefore able to let it go and fully enjoy the moment free of worry. I then thought to myself, *That's what faith looks like: a letting go of fear and falling into the arms of Jesus, come what may.*

Faith—that elusive sense of well-being for which each of us longs and seeks whenever we face unexpected or frightening news. Faith is the intersection of well-being and peace that reigns in our hearts and minds, despite harrowing circumstances or the dreaded unknown. While this is good to understand, how do we actually get to that place of peace?

Think back to my domino scenario. Consider how in the same way that one tiny bit of pressure administered in just the right way (or wrong way!) can trigger unwanted changes into our lives, so can one person (Jesus) trigger blessed changes. Certainly, when we are faced with unwanted and terrifying news, our emotions respond in kind. Hearing that my husband had cancer didn't have me jumping for joy. It had me on my knees. If I had continued to allow my fearful imaginings to grow, I would have been undone by all the what-ifs. Instead, by God's grace, I was reminded (through the Scripture I have read, studied, and memorized) of his faithful and constant love for me—and my husband.

Just as one phone call, conversation, letter, or text can serve to shatter our world, Jesus is the One Blessed Controller who can (and will) steady us as our life shifts and shakes beneath our feet. God's part is to be in control over every detail of our lives. Our part is to trust him with every detail of our lives. The strain comes when we attempt to wrestle with God over who is in control. As I willingly surrender to God's perfect plan for me, his grace floods in like a mighty stream, as does his peace that passes all understanding.

On that snowy, windy, and overall blustery day en route to the hospital, Jim and I both quieted our souls by asking the Lord to rule over the morning as he saw fit. We asked him to guide the surgeon's hands, give him divine wisdom, and help us forget about ourselves while we were there, so that we could be a blessing to others. Does that final request seem out of place? After all, my husband did have cancer and I am his spouse. Still, we have learned over the years that in the thick of the hardest and most terrifying moments, the best way to "get through" is to focus on meeting the needs of others. God's part plus our part equals faith and peace and grace enough for any and every storm of life.

## Take-away Action Thought

When my life takes a sudden and scary turn, I will do my part by meditating on Scripture and praying for a robust faith to overcome any and all fears, confident that God hears me when I call.

## My Heart's Cry to You, O Lord

Father, when I received this news, I felt my heart begin to beat faster and harder than is good for this body of mine. I don't want to react to bad news in a way that causes me to doubt you and your perfect provision for my life. Help me to take captive all thoughts and imaginings that rise up within me. My part is to discipline my wayward imaginings that tempt me to distrust your plan for my life. I bring you all my worries. I lay them at your feet and ask you to cover me with your perfect peace, today and forevermore. Amen.

## Faith Steps

1. Do a topical search through the Bible to read as many verses as you can that include the word *faith* in them to better understand it really means.
2. Once you have found three verses on faith that stand out to you, write them on cards to carry with you throughout the day.
3. Each evening this week, review your three faith verses and share their encouraging truths with at least one other person.

 # Chapter 2

## Trusting God with the Uncertainties of Life

Blessed are all who take refuge in him.

Psalm 2:12b

*We like to serve from the power position. We'd rather be healthy, wealthy, and wise as we minister to the sick, poor, and ignorant. But people hear the gospel best when it comes from those who have known difficulty. If we preach God's Word yet have little personal familiarity with suffering, the credibility gap makes it difficult to speak into others' lives. But our suffering levels the playing field.*

Randy Alcorn

After yet another long, lingering, cloud-covered winter where we transitioned immediately from cold to hot, I was ready for a sunny, relaxing summer to begin. But God had other plans. That sentence alone puts the fear of God into my heart and soul, because the closer I edge toward the age of sixty, I know from experience that God most often uses pain, suffering, and unexpected upsets (of all sizes, shapes, and colors) to mold me into the image of Jesus.

The happily naive and ever hopeful me began marking off the days on the calendar as I anticipated June, July, and

August—the months when my husband has a reprieve from teaching and coaching. Summer contains those precious days and weeks when we squeeze in fun and frivolity with family and friends on a more consistent basis. June, however, began with an early morning voice mail from my father who wanted me to call him as soon as possible. Nothing like receiving a cryptic voice mail first thing in the day to get one's heart rate rising. The long and the short of it was that my eighty-year-old mother had three brain aneurysms, one of which had just burst and all three of which would eventually require brain surgeries. Following the ten days my mother first spent in the ICU, she had six weeks to recover before the second surgery could take place. That almost fatal incident (and others like it) has been descriptive of my life for the past several years. Thankfully, my mom fared well after each of her procedures, which was a "miracle" according to her surgeon and the other medical professionals who took such wonderful care of her at the hospital.

To be precise, our family has grieved the loss of two dear loved ones who took their own lives, leaving family and friends struggling to make sense of the immensity of their pain that compelled them to completely despair of life. My son moved across the country and his recent wedding landed right after my mom's first brain aneurysm surgery and ICU stint. For my part, I was experiencing troubling physical symptoms that required multiple uncomfortable (painful!) tests to determine the problem and remedy. Freakishly, I somehow contracted cellulitis in my index finger after I pricked it on a thorn while weeding. This required yet another powerful course of strong antibiotics. All the while, my two primary freelance jobs ceased due to editorial and magazine shifts. To say that I felt a sense of free falling in every area of life is an understatement.

Just as I was regaining my emotional equilibrium, one of my dearest friends broke her hip right after we had attended an evening baseball game. I woke the next morning to a distressing phone message telling us that my friend had fallen in the parking lot minutes after we had said goodbye and was in a local hospital awaiting hip surgery. The painful irony is that my friend and I had been discussing how difficult aging is, and she had just undergone a DEXA scan that very morning to determine if her osteoporosis had progressed. Honestly, because of the circumstances, I felt a bit shell-shocked myself about the whole situation as I was again reminded of the frailty of life.

Each of these situations contains their own specific challenges and solutions. Alone, any one of them may be considered traumatic. Adding all these scenarios together is what tips a normally cool, calm, and collected woman over the edge. Physically. Emotionally. Mentally. Spiritually. To be clear, I thought I was handling everything (and everyone) just fine, thank you very much—until I began waking up in the middle of night with heart palpitations coupled with feeling irritable and sometimes weepy during the day. This told me that I needed to rest and regroup. Easier said than done when you're (A) a woman and (B) a caregiver. But these are exactly the moments when God reminds me (again and again and again) that he isn't counting on my strength to cope and get the job done. Instead, I'm counting on *his* power and strength to see me through today—and all my tomorrows.

I often refer back to the quotation above by Randy Alcorn because I need frequent reminders of its truth. We all want to love, serve, and minister to those around us from the "power position." We want (expect?) to be healthy, wealthy, and wise as we seek to meet the various needs of those we love. But in the real world, God often allows us to suffer some pain ourselves and endure seasons of genuine weakness, smack-dab in the middle of our responsibilities and callings. I really hate it when that happens!

I truly want to be able to give my best in service to others, but please don't expect me to serve while I'm sick, weak, emotionally drained, or feeling not up to the task. When I'm bombarded by bad news from every side, I long for God to shelter me in his loving arms. The last thing I want is to sense that God is nudging me out into the battlefield of service. But I've learned something in the past several years. There are seasons of rest, and everyone needs them. Then there are seasons of service, when we are forced to lean in hard to receive the grace that God promises and put the full weight of our trust in him as we seek to meet others' needs through God's strength and power alone.

In those situations where we are called on to go beyond what we believe we are capable of doing, we activate and strengthen our faith muscles, which I believe pleases God. I have to ask myself if I truly believe the promises God has made to supply all my needs (Phil. 4:19), not in a purely material sense but in regards to giving me the strength to serve despite my inherent weaknesses. This begs the next question: Do I trust God with the uncertainties of life? Only when I accept what God allows (the good, bad, and unexpected) and trust him to be the Blessed Controller of all things can I sleep in peace and wake with the confidence that God is and always will be my shelter in the time of storm. Because he is and because he always will be.

 *Take-away Action Thought*

When I feel overwhelmed by unexpected pain and suffering, I will grab hold of a promise from God that will remind me that he promises to never leave me or forsake me.

## My Heart's Cry to You, O Lord

Father, only you can fully understand how hard these past months have been and how shaky I feel inside. Each day, I expect to hear another tragic story or another heartbreaking scenario of loss and suffering. Please shelter my heart and mind against evil ponderings. Help me to follow your command in Philippians 4 to think about what is true, right, noble, pure, lovely, admirable, excellent, and praiseworthy. I cannot change these life events, but I can choose to focus on you and your promises. I choose to rest in you. Amen.

## Faith Steps

1. Search for God's promises that reassure you that he is your shelter in stormy times. Write out verses to carry with you today.
2. Look for someone who needs the same kind of encouragement and share the verses with them via e-mail, phone, or text.
3. Today, make a list of ten specific accounts of God's faithfulness to you and review it every day this week. Choose to be a good remember-er of all that God has done for you.

# Chapter 3

## Your Plan, God's Portion

God is our refuge and strength, an ever-present help in
trouble. Therefore we will not fear, though the earth give
way and the mountains fall into the heart of the sea.

Psalm 46:1–2

*Sometimes we need to trust God and rely on Him
to help us deal with the things we hate.*

*Linda Dillow*

The day before Thanksgiving, my dear friend Deb sent me
a text message to say that she was spending the day with
her twelve-year-old granddaughter, Ella, baking pies for
the holiday. I silently read Deb's text and thought, *How nice.
Grandma Deb is teaching her granddaughter Ella to bake.* Then,
it hit me: Ella is blind, so how can she bake? Moments later,
Deb sent me some lovely photos of Ella kneading and rolling
out pie dough, followed by pictures of finished products from
past baking adventures. They were beautiful!

All afternoon, as I was in my kitchen preparing for our
own Thanksgiving meal, my mind kept returning to the scene
I imagined with Deb and Ella: My good friend and her beloved

granddaughter in the kitchen baking, laughing, and creating wonderful memories together.

While today may indeed be beautiful for them now, Ella and her family had suffered through a rough beginning. I remember listening to Deb describe the heartbreaking scene she had experienced when her daughter gave birth to and the nurses swiftly whisked the baby away. She knew in that moment something was wrong. A short while later, the doctor came in and explained that Ella was born with a condition called bilateral anophthalmia. In layman's terms, Ella had been born without eyes.

During those first hours and days, Deb and her husband, Skip, along with Ella's parents and their entire extended family, were torn between grief and shock. All the hopes and dreams that parents store up in their hearts before a precious baby comes into this world vanished when Ella was born. Of course, they still loved this precious baby girl, but they hated the thought of what she would have to face every day of her life.

For Deb's family, as would be expected, they had been excited about the birth of this child, anticipating a healthy baby. When instead the baby was born with this physical disability, they then had to look to what God's portion was for them. Linda Dillow talks about our plans versus what God gives us—our plans but God's portion—which ties in with the quote at the beginning of this chapter. As we grow older, we begin to accept whatever God portions out to us, even when we hate it. Can anyone deny the deep struggle between these two opposing realities? Was there ever a more compelling illustration for Linda Dillow's insightful words cited above? "Sometimes we have to trust God and rely on Him to help us deal with the things we hate." Deb and her family did just that—and it was beautiful.

Where do you go for comfort and peace when your plan conflicts with God's portion? How do you cope with the unexpected that devastates you and your plans for the future? How can any of us find inner peace when circumstances beyond our control begin swirling around our feet, threatening to pull us into the depth of despair? We start with our faces on the floor before our all-powerful, all-loving, heavenly Father who promises us in Psalm 46 that he is our refuge, he is our strength, he is present, he is near, and he is here. And it's indeed beautiful.

For those of us who are Christ followers, we know in our heart of hearts that God loves us, because he sacrificed his beloved Son for us. As sisters and brothers of Christ, we instinctively know to lean in all the harder to God when the unthinkable assails us. Our emotions may very well ride the powerful tide that rushes in all around us as we attempt to cope with God's portion for us. The Lord understands our emotional struggles to accept these difficult circumstances. He doesn't condemn us for feeling our feelings, but he wants more for us in the face of our suffering than to drown in our emotional despair.

As we meditate on Psalm 46, these powerful truths about who God promises to be for us in the midst of any detour from our well-laid plans is, well, powerful. Our Father states, without exception, that he is our refuge when life terrifies us. He is our strength when we don't have the energy to take even a single step. He is present with us day and night, never leaving us alone. He is nearer to us than any human being ever could be. He is with us, inside of us, surrounding us with exactly what we need to handle the portion he has handpicked for us.

In a perfect world, our plans and God's portion would always meet hand in hand. As children of God in this broken world, we must learn to trust our heavenly Father even with what we hate (sickness, death, divorce, abandonment, disability, job loss, loneliness, depression, despair, war, racism, violence, and so on). Our Lord supplies us with exactly what we need to carry on through our suffering (grace, strength, power, love, joy, humility, compassion, perseverance, goodness, and so on). In this hurting world, only believers can see past suffering into the possibilities of redemption and restoration from God's loving hands. And it is beautiful.

## Take-away Action Thought

When God's portion differs from my plans, I will immediately turn my heart and mind toward his promises in Psalm 46 and meditate on these truths.

## My Heart's Cry to You, O Lord

Father, at this moment, when my emotions scream for relief and my mind resists your portion for me, I need your calming grace to help me surrender to your will for my life in this situation. My emotions are unsettled and nothing within me wants to walk this path you have set before me. Help me, please. Help me to lean in close to your loving embrace and sense your presence. I want to honor you by trusting you with this thing I hate, but I can't do it without your supernatural work deep within my heart and mind. I will sit here in silence as I meditate on your promises to be my refuge and my strength, as you do your perfect work in my heart so that I will not give way to fear. Amen.

## Faith Steps

1. Make a list of plans you have made in the past and how God intervened to steer your path to a better (or different) place. Then write out what you have learned from those experiences.

2. In your journal, create a column titled "My Plans" and a second one titled "God's Portion." In the coming days, when you face a hard situation or difficulty that was not in your plans, fill out specific responses of faith that will honor God in response to the portion God is allowing.

3. As a Bible memory exercise, meditate and memorize the first two verses of Psalm 46 so that when you are faced with the unexpected, you will not be afraid.

# Chapter 4

## When the Process Is Part of the Healing

He says, "Be still, and know that I am God."
Psalm 46:10

*I have difficulty sitting down and being quiet. When
a problem erupts in my life, I want to take action! I
want to DO something—anything—but be still.*

Linda Dillow

The first quarter of this year began the same way that last
year ended: busy, busy, busy! Life was setting a brisk pace
for me and my husband, Jim, and our adult children. I
recall the early months of this year as ones that were uncharacteristically hectic and demanding. When spring arrived and my
schedule showed no signs of slowing, I remember telling Jim
that I wasn't sure I could keep working at this pace much longer.
I truly felt like that famous hamster running around and around
on a stationary wheel—going ever faster but getting nowhere
at all. Something needed to change. And God made sure it did.

By the end of May, I still had a crazy-hectic schedule. But
in my defense, I'll say here that some of what I was dealing
with was not "a mess of my making," so to speak. Rather, the

early months of summer brought our entire family into more than one emergency room scenario that only added to my stress level. In a matter of a single week, my thirty-plus years of freelancing as a book reviewer for two magazines abruptly ceased. As a freelance writer/reviewer/author, I've had occasional work assignments through the years, but these two long-term assignments were steady income sources I counted on, perhaps even took for granted and lived with as part of my day-to-day work existence. So when they both ended at the same time, I felt unmoored, a bit grief-stricken, and more than a little shocked.

The best way to describe what I felt was "career grief." I soon recognized that much of my identity was wrapped up in my work. I was a reviewer. It wasn't just something I did. Per my usual response to any unwanted changes in my life, I began putting out the word to editors, colleagues, and magazines for which I had written in the past, letting them know I was looking for work to replace the freelance positions I had lost. In the midst of my job hunt, I sensed God telling me to stop working so hard at trying to find new work.

My inner response to this nudging was to question how that "cease striving and be still" *modus operandi* made any sense at all. I was a full-time reviewer, had been and always would be. End of story. Of course, when new reviewing doors weren't opening, I had to start listening more intently to what God was trying to teach me. Over the weeks that eventually led to months, my heart finally stopped grieving and began healing. I then felt God was teaching me that this sudden change in work status was his way of forcing me to be still—for my own good. After the initial sting wore off, I realized that given my lifelong track record and my personality, I never would have willingly given up those freelance assignments. God had to take them from me for my good.

I wonder how many of us have experienced the nudging in our hearts and minds from God that something needed to change in our lives but we quickly hushed it away. Change is hard—even change that does a good work within us. Change is unsettling—even change that forces us to cling all the more tightly to the Lord. Change is uncomfortable—even change that brings us to a place of greater maturity and grace.

Looking back, I remember one particularly puzzling afternoon when I felt angry and anxious about losing my work assignments. I felt such angst in my soul, and I wanted to stop being upset about matters that were beyond my control. As I prayed for God to do what he wanted to do with me and teach me whatever lesson I needed to learn so I could get on with my life, I sensed him telling me that the process was part of the healing.

*Hm*, I thought to myself, *the process was part of the healing?* So that meant that all the emotions, the lack of writing work, even the inner puzzling over these strange circumstances, were part of what God wanted me to experience and learn? I thought and I prayed some more, asking God to grant me the wisdom to see all that had transpired. I went back to Scripture verses that confirmed what I already knew: God loves me and wants only the best for me. He wants me to trust him, even though I don't understand. God wants me to believe he will provide for my needs. Perhaps most of all, I need to be fine with "being still and knowing he is God." Something needed to change, and God made sure it did. Praise him!

## Take-away Action Thought

When I face an unwanted or unsettling change in my life, I will resist every urge to frantically attempt to take control of the situation. Instead, I will discipline myself to sit quietly before the Lord so he can speak his comforting truth into my heart and mind.

## My Heart's Cry to You, O Lord

Father, you already know what my first response is going to be given any circumstance. My heart and mind struggle to slow down, to be calm, and to be still in your presence. But that is exactly what I need most. My urgent and habitual rush to change a circumstance or take control of an unwanted situation is actually *not* the most pressing need I have. Help me to discipline myself to sit down and quietly wait for you to communicate your eternal truth to my heart and mind. Nothing that happens to me is a surprise to you. Absolutely nothing. Give me your divine wisdom to know how to proceed when the time comes. But until I have peace within me, help me to be still and know that you are God. Amen.

## Faith Steps

1. Your first and best reaction to receiving difficult news should be to grab your Bible and journal and then begin to write out Scripture verses that bring specific comfort to you in the face of unwanted change.

2. Spend time at least twice a day (morning and evening) meditating on the verses you have selected so that they are never far from your thoughts.

3. Pray these verses back to God with the confidence that he never makes a promise he will not keep. Share your worries with a friend and ask that person to keep you accountable as you work through your struggles over these changes.

# Chapter 5

## Keeping an Account of God's Faithfulness

Cast all your anxiety on him because he cares for you.
1 Peter 5:7

*No person on this side of eternity lives a fear-free life. No*
*one always operates out of the rest and security of faith in*
*God. Every one of us has moments in which we lose our mind*
*and our way. So here is the thing we must fight against:*
*we must not allow fear to become the lens through which*
*we view life and the guide for how we make decisions.*

Paul David Tripp

*O*ne Sunday morning, our pastor was concluding a series
from the book of Judges that focused on Samson's life
and his eventual demise because of his lifelong struggle
with lust. As he summed up Samson's decision-making process,
a faulty one to be sure most of the time, our pastor made a statement that started me thinking deeply about how individuals
fall prey to sin and temptation, in large part because they feel
through their problems rather than seek God's direction.

Unpacking a bit from this biblical character's eventual slav-
ery and then death, I wondered how often I speak the words

*I feel* when I would fare better saying (and thinking), "It is written." After all, Jesus countered Satan's temptations, not by his emotions but by repeating what God had said.

On the way home from the service and then on into the afternoon, I kept reflecting on the news our close friends received not so long ago. Their child had been struggling in school and they finally had her tested. To their shock and dismay, the tests determined their little girl had a low I.Q. So low, in fact, that it was a real possibility that their daughter would never be able to live independently.

As our friends began to work through this devastating news, I watched them move from fear as the unknown future gave way to the what-if questions for which there weren't any answers, to finally, a calm acceptance. Since I almost always picture myself in my friends' situations and contemplate how I would handle what they are facing, I was eager to ask them how they worked through their shock and fear of the future. What they said amazed me. "For every 'I feel . . .' there is an 'It is written' found in Scripture. Our responsibility is to run to the promises of God so that our emotions don't run us to the ground."

*It is written.* If you are like me, you pay special attention to the red-letter words of Jesus found throughout the New Testament in some Bibles. If Jesus said it, then I better pay attention to it. Not only did Jesus quote Scripture to refute temptation, he frequently used specific Old Testament accounts to teach his followers how to live as overcomers in a broken, sinful world. I'm reminded that one of the primary and persistent sins the Israelites committed was that of forgetting all God had done for them.

Of course, we can easily judge the Israelites for their short memories and shortsightedness in decision-making. But are we really so different? After all, the majority of our first responses to troubling news are generally fear-based ones. Some frightening report comes our way and before we even end the call or read the entire e-mail or text, we've initiated damage control. I can only imagine Jesus shaking his head sadly and saying to us, "This, my child, is not how I want you to respond." I can envision him sitting down next to me with an open Bible in hand, leading me page by page to those passages of Scripture that offer specific comfort for my specific problem.

It *is* written—for my blessing, encouragement, and lifelong benefit. God has supplied all I need to learn to think my way through my fearful struggles. My part is to immerse myself in God's promises and make them my own. When I am facing a fear-full situation, I will be best equipped to get through unscathed if I first run to God's promises and then take time to remember all he has already done for me.

## *Take-away Action Thought*

Because I know how easy it is for my emotions to rule me, I will choose to become a student of God's word daily and become a good remember-er of his faithfulness to me.

## *My Heart's Cry to You, O Lord*

Father, my emotions are so out of control at this moment that I can hardly calm myself down enough to take a deep breath. I need your comfort and calming presence to help me settle down.

I have decisions to make, and I'm so upset that I don't think I can trust myself to choose wisely. Please, Lord, lead me to those eternal promises from your word that will provide me with peace, wisdom, and security. I long for you to make yourself known to me right now, so that I will have the strength to face my enemy. Help me to remember all you have done in the past so that I can more easily rest in your provision for me. Amen.

## Faith Steps

1. When you start to feel overwhelmed or afraid, make a list of "I feel" and "It is written" statements that counter your out-of-control emotions. When you face something that frightens you, refer back to this list and pray through it.
2. Today, ask a trusted friend to pray for you and with you that you would be consistent in spending time daily in God's word and praying through verses that encourage you to trust in his provision.
3. Every day this week for thirty minutes, put on praise music and then write down in your journal how this time of worship has helped you focus on Jesus rather than on your fears.

# Chapter 6

## Finding Your Purpose

Trust in the Lord with all your heart and lean not
on your own understanding; in all your ways submit
to him, and he will make your paths straight.

Proverbs 3:5–6

*All of your abilities—and your disabilities—were created
to fit the unique plan God has for you. No one can fulfill
your purpose but you. And God's plan for you and His plan
for me embrace far more than the events or circumstances
that happen to us. They also embrace what God wants us to
be and do and what He desires to do in and through us.*

*Linda Dillow*

*O*ver the years, I've sat through more graduation cer-
emonies than I honestly care to remember. Most of
them, I'm sad to report, didn't keep my attention long
enough to have been able to offer any kind of meaningful take-
away life challenge. There is, however, always a first time for
everything. In mid-November, our family sat on stiff-as-a-board
folding chairs in a nondescript gymnasium, awaiting our young-
est daughter's walk across the stage as one of the graduating
students receiving a master's degree in social work.

Before the processional started, I had perused the commencement program, secretly wondering how long this particular graduation ceremony would last. What I didn't anticipate was how absolutely riveting (and eternally applicable) the commencement speaker's address would be to me personally. This gentleman opened his speech by reciting the Lord's Prayer and then transitioned immediately into discovering the purpose of life for these graduates. In truth, the speaker's words resonated deeply within my heart.

The speaker stated that every one of us should continually reflect on the life we desire to live. Our hearts will affect our desires. Our desires will affect our choices. Our choices will affect the impact our lives can have on others. Rather than focusing on getting the best job available, he challenged, set your focus on becoming the best person you can be. Today, on graduation day, most folks view it as the end of something. Instead, view graduation day as the first day that God calls you out into the world in the ministry of reconciliation and redemption. He concluded by saying it matters little what job one lands in, because God's highest purpose for each of his children is to prayerfully and actively seek to bring others into relationship with Jesus Christ no matter what their job description.

I know I wasn't the only one in the audience who felt the power and inspiration behind this commencement speaker's words. As soon as he bowed his head to pray in closing, the audience cheered. I felt energized to go out and make my own mark on the world, just as the young graduates did!

Who would have guessed that the rousing words of a college commencement speaker would so affect both the young and the old in the audience? Certainly not me. And yet, the lesson we gleaned that chilly November morning gave way to other introspective ponderings in the weeks to come. As so many graduates like my daughter have happily anticipated moving directly from their graduation ceremony into gainful employment in their particular field of study, the hard reality is it takes time, work, and ample amounts of patience before that desire is realized.

So what happens when we diligently labor and prepare for the vocational purpose (or ministry) for which we believe God has designed us, but it doesn't materialize? Or at least, it doesn't materialize as quickly as we had hoped? At this juncture, and I believe the speaker would agree, you must "trust in the Lord with all your heart and lean not on your own understanding; in all your ways submit to him, and he will make your paths straight." Our keenest desires, hopes, and dreams need to be surrendered to the perfect plan and perfect timing of God.

Certainly, as we wait, we apply ourselves to waiting well by daily studying God's word and meditating on his promises. We work while we wait. Not perhaps in our chosen field of study, but we work nonetheless until God opens the right position (or ministry) for us. We remind ourselves again and again that our overarching purpose in life as Christ followers is not to be defined by our occupation or job status. Rather, we have a lifelong and eternal ministry of reconciliation and redemption to pursue that is far more encompassing than any job we may land.

Yes, we must hold fast to the important biblical mandate of sharing our faith in Jesus Christ and his ministry of reconciliation with sinners. God can and will use our talents, gifts, experience, and knowledge to serve his purpose. Just as I was challenged along with every other Christ follower, I must never forget that no matter how my job description may alter through the years, my life purpose remains the same: to be an ambassador of the kingdom of God.

### Take-away Action Thought

When my life's plans seem to stall out before my eyes and I don't understand what God is doing, I will take myself back to Scripture and spend time reading Jesus' commands to his disciples. I will remind myself that my overall purpose in life is to minister to others so that they are drawn to Jesus as their Savior.

### My Heart's Cry to You, O Lord

Father, I need your eternal perspective in my life right now as I fight daily against discouragement and the temptation to give up. I worked so hard to prepare for the vocation and ministry to which I believe you have called me. And yet, I find myself waiting and wondering when that position will open up for me. Help me to remember that you are in control of all things and that you want what is best for me. In this time of waiting, when I feel as though nothing is happening, give me the hope I need to start each new day happy and resolved to work hard and share your amazing love with every person with whom I come into contact. Amen.

### Faith Steps

1. Young or old, God has given every child of his the Great Commission to spread the good news of Jesus Christ.

Read and reread the words of Jesus that he spoke to his disciples and memorize verses that will fortify you during this time of waiting.

2. As you wait, look for fresh opportunities to serve and give of your time and talents so that you can make full use of each day.

3. No matter what season of life you are in, God is calling you to make the most of your hours and days. Spend time in prayer asking God to bring specific people or service possibilities to mind and then take the necessary steps to be of use.

# Chapter 7

## Limitations Do Not Define You

"The thief comes only to steal and kill and destroy; I have
come that they may have life, and have it to the full."

John 10:10

*It's easy and quite normal to take on our difficulty as
our identity. Whether it's the loss of a loved one, the
betrayal of a friend, physical sickness, or financial
ruin, no hardship in this fallen world has the power
to define you or determine your potential.*

*Paul David Tripp*

Annie, my eighty-year-old friend, once described to
me how she refused to allow her advancing health
restrictions to diminish her ability to make a difference. "I can no longer travel overseas to serve as a missionary," she said. "But I can serve within my city. I will soon no
longer drive around town, but I can call and write letters to
bring encouragement. I will eventually no longer be able to use
a telephone because of my hearing loss or write because my
hand trembles, but I can pray. So I will pray day and night for
every person I used to minister to in person." Hearing Annie

say this made me wonder if perhaps we take the wrong view of physical limitations. It seems that God can certainly help us find a way around them.

I've thought about Annie's remarkable words and have been challenged by her resilient spirit. Even though many of her life's plans were cut short by health issues that reduced her once physically strong self to a frail woman, nothing robbed Annie of her heart. As her body grew weaker, she never allowed the personal disappointment she endured to steal from her the purpose for which Jesus intended her to fulfill.

Certainly, failing health meant no more overseas missionary work, but Annie adjusted her vision to match her abilities. When Annie ceased foreign missions, she went local. When she couldn't safely drive any longer, Annie ministered from home. Even when her body became too weak to call or write, she prayed. As Annie's world of ministry necessarily shrunk because of her physical frailty, her inner world of faith grew in similar proportions—deeper and wider. Annie held loosely to her dreams, surrendering each one at the foot of the cross. God continued to show Annie new ways as to how she could use her gifts and talents to serve others.

At first glance, Annie's life might appear to be a series of one disappointment after another. But it wasn't. Early on when her health began to fail, Annie determined that she would not fall victim to Satan's scheme to steal, kill, or destroy her or the life that Jesus had paid the ultimate price to redeem. Instead, she took her losses to Jesus every time, finding that he gave her endless opportunities to share his perfect love in ways she never anticipated.

When we face physical, mental, or emotional limitations, it can be scary. And sad. And hard. And disappointing. The list can go on and on. Aging itself is risky business, because we are forced to face the truth that even though we might feel young on the inside, our physical body reminds us in countless uncomfortable and painful ways that we are getting older. From our day-to-day activities and responsibilities to carry out those often overwhelming, unexpected challenges that leave us feeling exhausted and undone, we must find faith-driven ways to accept our limitations. For some, limitations may not present themselves in a purely physical sense. Perhaps we find ourselves with limited material resources, limited housing, limited mobility, or limited relationally. Again, the list can go on and on. The point is that we must take our limitations (or losses) to the Lord and seek his wisdom for redeeming each one. Yes, it's inconvenient and it's uncomfortable. It's humbling to face our inadequacies. But Jesus made it clear that if we give way to the enemy's subtle message that our lives no longer matter, then we are forgetting that Jesus came to give us life—life to the full. We need to remember that our identity is eternally secure in the person of Jesus Christ. As Tripp reminds us, "No hardship in this fallen world has the power to define you or determine your potential." No matter how limited we become, we serve an unlimited God with an eternal plan—of which we are a part.

## Take-away Action Thought

When life suddenly changes and my dreams and desires have to be set aside because of limitations, I will not despair. I will remind myself that nothing that happens in this broken world can define the identity I have as one of God's beloved children. Even though I may become physically limited and my life's goals become diminished, I serve an unlimited God who gives me life eternal and life to the full.

## My Heart's Cry to You, O Lord

Father, in this season of my life, I am experiencing unexpected and—honestly—unwanted limitations of all sorts. In my heart of hearts, you know that my desire is to serve you by being active in my community. I want to be among the people you've called me to love and serve, but my strength is gone and my stamina is depleted. I don't know if I will ever recover fully from this season where I'm becoming more and more accustomed to having to say no to others. Help me to find the new normal in my life and recognize what I can do to serve. Open my heart and eyes to those people to whom you want to me to minister and then show me how to accomplish this. Never let me sit home and pity myself because I can't do what I once did. Fill me with your Spirit and let my heart soar toward heaven in prayer. Amen.

## Faith Steps

1. When you are faced with significant and possibly permanent life limitations, do not give way to self-pity. Instead, pray and ask God to show you new opportunities to serve others.

2. Ask your closest friends to pray with you as you seek to accept your new normal, and ask them to keep you accountable as you wait on the Lord to show you what your life may look like in the coming days.

3. This week, spend time praying every day for each person to whom you used to be able to minister when you were stronger. Don't forget their needs even though you may no longer have the opportunity to visit them in person. Your daily act of service will be acting as a prayer warrior on their behalf.

# Chapter 8

## Living This Day Regret Free

"Forget the former things; do not dwell on the
past. See, I am doing a new thing! Now it springs
up; do you not perceive it? I am making a way in
the wilderness and streams in the wasteland."

Isaiah 43:18–19

*In the total expanse of human life, there is not a
single square inch of which Christ, who alone is
sovereign, does not declare, "That is mine!"*

*Abraham Kuyper*

Only later could I laugh when I read this quotation by
Abraham Kuyper. That's because when I first read it,
my situation was anything but comical.

Seven months ago, Jim and I purchased a dilapidated house
in the city to renovate. Since then, every day after Jim finishes
his long day teaching mathematics at the local high school, he
heads over to "the house" (as we've come to call it), where he
spends at least two or more hours working room by room to
make the uninhabitable habitable once again.

Jim has chosen to do the majority of the repairs himself for several reasons, but his self-imposed primary rule was to not hire out what he has the skills to do. Given that premise, he has been working every day, including weekends, to complete the house before the six-month deadline the bank assigned him. We have both been anticipating getting "the house" done so that we could sell or rent it. As the finish line approached, Jim had been looking a lot happier in recent weeks. That was before the electrical mishap set him back days.

It was just one of those unseen setbacks that happens often enough, but once in play sets in motion a whole series of costly repercussions in money and time. And then, of course, there's the regret. Why did he choose to drill in that particular section of the wall? Why didn't he drill one inch lower? Why did the former owners seal off the electrical outlet? Why didn't he notice the slanted wire before he drilled? Why? Why? Why? Regret. Regret. Regret.

These were the thoughts and sentiments he shared with me when it first happened and then every day afterward that he had to spend correcting his mistake. Before this happened, everything seemed to be going so smoothly and Jim was pretty sure the inspection would pass with no hitches. But after electric sparks started flying and a minor fire started inside the wall of the living room, Jim assessed the damage after he put out the fire. Although it could have been much worse, Jim hadn't anticipated that drilling in that specific square inch would set in motion a whole series of new repairs (not when he had tightly calculated everything he needed to get done in time for the inspection). Now he had even more to do to get past this glitch and still make his deadline.

But it was during those additional work hours that he realized that his time belongs to the Lord, and so does his work. His efforts and accomplishments also belong to the God. This is the same for everyone everywhere. All time, work, efforts, and accomplishments belong indeed to the Lord. As Abraham Kuyper wrote (and now you'll understand why I laughed), "There is not a *single square inch* of which the Christ, who alone is sovereign, does not declare, 'That is mine!'"

Time is that elusive entity we all struggle to make the most of but find difficult to relinquish into our sovereign Lord's care and keeping. With the deepest of regrets, we tend to rehearse over and over again those mistakes that have cost us the most. In some instances, these mistakes are costly in both time and money. At other times, our missteps cost us relationally or vocationally. Whatever the cost, the Lord wants us to learn from the past so that we do not repeat our errors. That's it. Learn from our mistakes so as to not repeat them.

Our task for today is to give our hours and minutes to the Lord in the morning when we arise and ask him to use our time (his time!) as he sees fit. As we step into our day, we also need to embrace the promise found in Isaiah 43:18–19: "Forget the former things; do not dwell on the past. See, I am doing a new thing! Now it springs up; do you not perceive it? I am making a way in the wilderness and streams in the wasteland." For each of us, our own personal "wasteland" of regrets is uniquely ours. Perhaps you have struggled with self-control. Then today is a new day for the Lord to impart the grace you need to exercise this. Possibly, your wasteland is how you handle close personal relationships. For you also, today is a new day for the Lord to provide the wisdom and understanding to nurture and develop healthy relationships.

Whatever our regrets, the Lord wants us to begin each new day hopeful, joyful, and resolved to embrace his grace and strength to set a new path for today and every day. Let go of regrets. Learn from past mistakes. Boldly proclaim God's promise to equip you to meet each day's challenges, with grace and strength to live regret free for these twenty-four hours.

### Take-away Action Thought

When I begin to feel paralyzed by my past mistakes and am mired in regret, I will read and meditate on Isaiah 43:18–19 until I understand its implications in my life. I will memorize these passages and say them out loud during the day whenever I start to fall into that pit of regret.

### My Heart's Cry to You, O Lord

Father, today I am struggling over my past mistakes. I keep revisiting the same painful memories and all the hurt I caused. I cannot lay blame for what happened at anyone's feet but my own. Still, I need to move forward in faith, believing that you will help me forge a new path today. Give me the grace and strength I need to press ahead and look back only to learn from my errors. I've spent too much time punishing myself. Today is a new day, and I want to live it full of hope and joy. Amen.

Living This Day Regret Free

## Faith Steps

1. Meditate and memorize Isaiah 43:18–19. Speak these verses out loud throughout the day to remind yourself that every morning starts a fresh beginning for you.

2. When you begin to fall into the pit of regret, drop to your knees and ask the Lord to surround you with his loving presence. Sit quietly before the Lord, contemplating his great love for you as evidenced by his sacrifice on the cross.

3. If you find yourself struggling to work through past mistakes, call on good friends to help you get past the past. Share honestly with them how you're feeling and what you're thinking. Then ask them to pray for you every day until your is only a distant memory.

# Chapter 9

## *Transforming Your Trials into Comfort for Others*

Praise be to the God and Father of our Lord Jesus
Christ, the Father of compassion and the God of
all comfort, who comforts us in all our troubles, so
that we can comfort those in any trouble with the
comfort we ourselves receive from God.

2 Corinthians 1:3–4

*This world, with all its evils, is God's deliberately
chosen environment for people to grow in their
characters. The character and trustworthiness we
form here, we take with us there, to Heaven.*

*Josef Tson*

*W*hile updating my yearly birthday calendar, I
was struck by how old everyone on my list was
growing—myself included! They're just numbers,
folks tell us. Until they're not. Growing older means increasing
occurrences of health difficulties, limitations (self-imposed
or not), and loss (family, friends, strength, stamina, abilities).
Some individuals choose not to accept these not-so-fun aspects
of growing older. They think that if they deny their true age,

then the challenges associated with growing older will cease
to exist as well!

On the flip side, aging has so many benefits, not the least of
which is character growth and trustworthiness not often found
in the young. Maturity also equips us to enter into the pain
and suffering of others around us. Why? Because we've been
there. When I look back to my younger twenty-something self
and remember hearing my mother lament about hot flashes and
sleepless nights, I felt so far removed from her physical problems that I just shrugged them off. I didn't have any comparable
grid that would help me understand her struggles. Today, some
thirty years later and having suffered for years with persistent
hot flashes, I get it. And now my empathy quotient is at its
maximum.

Thankfully, my own four pregnancies were problem free.
When friends endured miscarriages, I felt sympathy and sad-
ness, but I couldn't fully enter into their pain. Then after two
of my daughters both miscarried twice and I experienced their
pain up close and personal, my response was quite different.
I've now learned how to grieve alongside other moms who have
miscarried. After suffering with my daughters as their mother
and as a grandmother, I get it.

When my children were young and their problems were
solvable, I hurt for those who had rebellious teens and young
adult children on the run from God; but I didn't fully grasp the
pain and sorrow these children's actions brought to a family.
Then my own daughter took a five-year wayward path, living
recklessly—dangerously even—and I finally understood these
parents' pain. After suffering alongside my husband, I got it.

Of course, although none of us wants to endure pain or
suffering, it is inevitable. As the Romanian pastor Josef Tson,
who suffered persecution in the Soviet Bloc, wrote, "This world,
with all its evils, is God's deliberately chosen environment for

people to grow in their characters. The character and trust-worthiness we form here, we take with us there, to Heaven." Yes, I get it.

Now that I do get it, I see that it's all worthwhile. The precious comfort of being able to bring comfort to others after we have suffered makes our own hardship and trials worth it. The truth is that we can't offer another sufferer the gentle wisdom and tender insight they need to journey through their ordeals unless we have been refined by suffering's fire ourselves. This is why in 2 Corinthians 1:3–4, Paul offers readers this rousing exhortation to take heart during their own seasons of suffering: "Praise be to the God and Father of our Lord Jesus Christ, the Father of compassion and the God of all comfort, who comforts us in all our troubles, so that we can comfort those in any trouble with the comfort we ourselves receive from God."

Talk about getting the most bang for your buck! If I'm going to suffer, I really want (1) to learn how to suffer well by leaning hard into the loving arms of my Savior, and (2) to pass on whatever comfort, hope, and encouragement I can to others who suffer after me. Rereading these verses in 2 Corinthians reassures me that my heavenly Father is a God of compassion and of comfort. He wants me to accept his compassion and comfort, because he loves me. In turn, I have the privilege of passing on this compassion and comfort to those who suffer around me. I am blessed so that I can be a blessing. It's a double blessing, and that works for me.

## Take-away Action Thought

When I am in the midst of suffering, I will turn my thoughts toward the compassionate and comforting God who is close by me. I will remind myself that God never wastes my pain and that he is doing a good work in my heart and mind, preparing me to be an able and competent comforter to others. I will also set my hope on the permanency of heaven as my ultimate home.

## My Heart's Cry to You, O Lord

Father, I need your wisdom and supernatural grace to help me reframe this pain and suffering into something good. I know you are with me, and I know you have great compassion for what I am going through. You love me, but I am a weak and frail vessel and can feel so discouraged. Will this trial ever end? I certainly pray it will. Until it does, however, give me your hour-by-hour grace to respond to this pain in a way that brings you glory. Help me, Lord, to trust you and let my faith grow all the stronger, so that I can be a source of comfort to others in the coming days. Amen.

## Faith Steps

1. During seasons of suffering, discipline yourself to meditate on 2 Corinthians 1:3–4. Read and reread this passage of Scripture until you are able to praise God in the midst of your pain, with the hope that he will use you as a comforter to others.

2. Contact three people this week you know are suffering and in need of encouragement, by visiting, calling, or writing a note.

3. Spend time daily in prayer, asking God to bring to mind those who need prayer. As the Lord leads, follow up with each person and make plans to offer some kind of practical assistance in the coming days.

# Chapter 10

## Stretching Yourself to Outdo Others in Love

Be devoted to one another in love. Honor one another
above yourselves. Never be lacking in zeal, but keep
your spiritual fervor serving the Lord. Be joyful in hope,
patient in affliction, faithful in prayer. Share with the
Lord's people who are in need. Practice hospitality.

Romans 12:10–13

*Kind hearts are quietly kind. They let the car cut into traffic
and the young mom with three kids move up in the checkout
lane. They pick up the neighbor's trashcan. And they are
especially kind at church. They understand that perhaps
the neediest person they'll meet all week is the one standing
in the foyer or sitting on the row behind them in worship.*

Max Lucado

ometimes God calls us to outdo one another in love,
although no one but you can know how costly that
single act of obedience may be to you. If you're like
me, you do a quick mental tabulation before committing to
give money, serve in a specific capacity, or even practice

hospitality. But last year, God kept impressing upon my heart the need to "be quietly kind," as Max Lucado puts it. It was one of the most difficult tests of obedience I've faced in a long time.

My emotions were highly charged over this matter, and I dreaded the very idea of initiating contact this person, let alone exhibit any kindness! But God nudged my heart day and night, until I surrendered my will to his. Looking back now, I'm so thankful I obeyed even though my heart wasn't "in" it.

While it may be easy to advise others to "let it go" when they ask us for advice, it can be torturous to apply those same principles to our own sticky situations. Case in point: I'd spent untold hours reading, reviewing, preparing interview questions, and then writing author interviews over a few months' span. I fully expected to be paid for my work, because I always had been paid by this publication. Then a buyout and change in management altered everything.

At first, I was happy enough to give the benefit of the doubt to them, given the necessary overlap of training and settling into new positions for this new managerial team. But after three months of little contact, I realized something was wrong. Finally, after five months, it was clear that no check was arriving in the mail, even though it had been promised multiple times. My heart struggled against being deceived, and my wallet felt the pinch of lost income. I prayed every day for the Lord to give me wisdom and keep me from growing bitter against this management team.

During one of my times of "storming the gates of heaven" with my cries of injustice, I sensed the Lord nudging me to forgive the employee with whom I had the most contact and to write her a kind and affirming note. My first reaction was a silent scream with vigorous heading shaking. Then, as always, the Holy Spirit began replaying various verses in my head about forgiveness and overcoming evil with good. He had me there.

Resolved to be obedient despite the perceived cost to my-self, I sat down before the Lord, committed to forgive them and let it go. To be honest, it was much easier to forgive what I assumed was mismanagement and a mistake than it was to forfeit my pay. I reminded myself from Psalm 24:1 that "the earth is the Lord's and everything in it, the world, and all who live in it," which helped me let it go for good. For my next task, I sat down and wrote an e-mail that was both kind and affirm-ing and then hit "send." I never heard back from the woman and I probably never will. But for my part, I did what the Lord required of me. I let it go.

If you are anything like me, the idea of being "quietly kind" is an attractive one. I'd like to come to the end of my life, look back, and believe I'd developed a consistent track record of being kind to others. I know I've made mistakes in judging others harshly and murmuring under my breath about people and situations I found inexplicably foolish. Then in the next breath, I've had to confess my sin and beg the Lord to give me the wisdom, understanding, and self-control to use my words in a way than honors him.

When we are faced with sticky situations with prickly people who tend to rub us the wrong way, it is all the more needful for us to rely on the supernatural grace and strength we require to exhibit unconditional love, by being "quietly kind" to those folks we find the most challenging. It is only when we can consistently reflect back on these tough life situations with people we struggle to love and understand that we can honestly say that we have stretched ourselves to outdo others in love. And yet that is precisely what this passage in Romans commands us as Christ followers to do. Today and every day. We need to honor one another above ourselves.

## Take-away Action Thought

When I am faced with a sticky situation with a person I find challenging to love or understand, I will pray and ask the Lord to give me concrete, doable ideas to express unconditional love toward them. I will also pray daily for divine wisdom, asking the Lord to help me better understand this person's inner struggles and burdens.

## My Heart's Cry to You, O Lord

Father, I'm in a quandary and not at all certain how I can show love or express kindness to a person I really do not care to be around. I wish I could honestly say that I find it easy to demonstrate unconditional love toward this individual, but I don't. Please help me to develop the compassionate caring attitude I need so that I can enter in and show love in a way that is both sincere and genuine. Help me to gently ask the questions that will reveal this person's need, and then help me to come up with ways to lighten their load. Amen.

## Faith Steps

1. Write down specific people you believe the Lord is nudging you to exhibit "quiet kindness" toward, and

then make a list of specific ways you can show unconditional love toward each person.

2. As you work through this list of people you find challenging to love or care for, ask the Lord to reveal to
your heart if you have failed to forgive them for a past
offence. If you have not forgiven something, then spend
all the time it takes before the Lord to confess this sin
of unforgiveness—and then forgive.

3. This week, prayerfully ask the Lord to help you to keep
stretching yourself out of your comfort zone, as you
enter into others' lives to serve and love them. Don't
stay inside your "safety zone," where it's easy to serve.
Allow the Lord to lead the way.

# Chapter 11

## Enter in (All the Way in)

> But he said to me, "My grace is sufficient for you, for
> my power is made perfect in weakness." Therefore
> I will boast all the more gladly about my weaknesses,
> so that Christ's power may rest on me.
>
> 2 Corinthians 12:9

> *Our weakness will not get in the way of what the*
> *Lord wants to do in us. Our delusions of strength*
> *will! The power of God is for the weak! The grace*
> *of God is for the unable! The promises of God are for*
> *the faint! The wisdom of God is for the foolish!*
>
> *Paul David Tripp*

*I* hate hospitals, and I cannot imagine ever choosing a
vocation that would require me to put in forty hours a
week, year after year, in a place surrounded by people
who are fighting to regain their health or battling for their lives.
I honestly believe I'm not made of stern enough stuff. Doesn't
everyone feel this way? The short answer is no, not everyone

is "highly allergic" to hospital settings, and I have family and friends who love working in these settings to prove it.

For the majority of folks, however, I still maintain that the sentiment of hating hospitals is true—for the simple reason that the only reason we go to a hospital is because we are sick or someone we care about is sick. The emotions that run high in hospital settings are fraught with fear, grief, and loss. No one really knows what the outcome will be when they are admitted to the hospital. I've lived long enough now to witness minor operations go wrong, with deadly consequences. I've also witnessed the most unlikely, precarious health scenarios surprise everyone, including the medical staff, with miraculous turn-around results.

This brings me full circle to the "I hate hospitals" sentiment. When I am faced with a medical condition that includes a medical procedure, I'm fully aware of my weakness and the frailty of life. When I'm asked to be that person waiting for news of a loved one in the OR, I'm similarly faced with the reality of their physical weakness and, again, the frailty of life.

Yet, and in spite of, these uncomfortable emotions that tug at my heart and mind, I know that God wants me to "enter in" to these tenuous situations with the boldness and confidence he supplies, but I still need some persuading. First, I have to be convinced beyond any doubt that God will give me the strength to face personally whatever he allows. Second, I have to be convinced beyond any doubt that God will give me the strength to come alongside and "enter in" to whatever pain and suffering my loved ones face. Truthfully, it's much easier to sit at home and hear about others' sorrow from a distance. You know it is. But God calls us to throw ourselves on his mercy (for the abiding strength we need) so that we can enter in (all the way in) to bear one another's burdens. Enter in. All the way in.

Another popular and equally troubling phrase is "I'm just not comfortable doing that," which begs the question, "Who is?" I doubt anyone is comfortable with the idea of having to offer deathbed condolences to a grieving family. I also cannot imagine anyone being comfortable with the thought of having to sit alongside a friend who is receiving a terminal cancer diagnosis, or being summoned to the home of a family member whose son just committed suicide. No one is comfortable with these emotionally harrowing experiences, but still we go.

This promise in 2 Corinthians 12:9—"My grace is sufficient for you, for my power is made perfect in weakness. Therefore I will boast all the more gladly about my weaknesses, so that Christ's power may rest on me"—reminds us that we don't have to be strong to enter in to another's suffering. Jesus' words make it clear that it is his strength (and his alone) that equips us to be ready comforters. Yet some believers balk. "I don't feel strong!" Of course, you don't. It's only when we take those first steps of obedience and "enter in" that God's strengthening power and grace for every situation overcomes us. So don't wait to feel comfortable, because you'll wait forever. Instead, pray for God's strength to supply your every need. Enter in. All the way in.

## Take-away Action Thought

When I am fraught with fear, knowing what I should do to be of help and comfort to another, I will pray and ask the Lord to give me his strengthening power. I will recite this verse from 2 Corinthians 12:9 over and over, until I have committed it to memory.

## My Heart's Cry to You, O Lord

Father, today I am feeling keenly aware of my own personal physical weakness and I'm struggling to find peace of mind. Not only am I aware of my own weakness, but I also feel ill equipped to offer comfort to a loved one who is suffering. I'm afraid of falling apart when we are together, or of not knowing the right words to say to bring encouragement. I know what 2 Corinthians 12:9 promises me, and I know that your strength will rest powerfully on me when I admit my own frailty and inabilities. Lord, I confess them freely. I need you and your supernatural power to fill me so that I can fully enter in to another's suffering. Amen.

## Faith Steps

1. Memorize 2 Corinthians 12:9 and spend time with the Lord, asking him to reveal any areas where you are struggling to accept your own weaknesses. Are you proud and independent? Or do you confess your weaknesses freely and accept the Lord's grace and strength into every area of your heart and mind?

2. During the next seven days, spend quiet time before the Lord, asking him to show you ways you can step into others' lives as a way of "entering in" and sharing their burdens with them.

3. Make contact with several good friends and ask them if you might get together once a month to pray for those in your lives in great need, and also develop a monthly plan to help these same individuals as a group.

# Chapter 12

## *Remaining Hopeful When Life Interrupts*

May these words of my mouth and this meditation of my heart
be pleasing in your sight, LORD, my Rock and my Redeemer.
Psalm 19:14

*You and I never live our lives alone. We bring a rich,
multifaceted inner world of thoughts, desires, and emotions
to every experience. We never leave alone anything that
happens to us or around us. We push everything in our lives
through our conceptual, emotional, spiritual grid. This
means that you're not just shaped by your experiences,
but you give shape to those experiences as well.*

*Paul David Tripp*

**W**e make some progress, but then an interruption
comes along and sets us back. It seems like it's
always a two-steps-forward-three-steps-backward
dance through life! Trying to make sense of this conundrum is
risky business. I witnessed this during a recent conversation
with two mothers who have adult sons struggling with addiction.
With tears in her eyes, one mom said that she was counting the
days until her son was officially clean for a full year. Just days

away from this momentous celebration for their family and my friend, she kept saying, "It's been almost a year . . . almost a year since he used." Her happy tears couldn't be contained.

The second mom sat nodding in agreement, grateful for her friend's words of thanksgiving about her son's sobriety. Then she said, "I'm so grateful that both of my sons are clean today." For this particular mother, her sons have been in and out of rehabilitation facilities, hospitals, and clinics, trying to get clean and stay that way. She was sincerely grateful that on this day both of her sons were (1) alive and (2) clean from the drugs. She doesn't look for borrowed trouble in the long tomorrows. Rather, she sets her mind on Jesus and hopes and prays for today.

I sat listening to these mothers elaborate on their journeys as parents who have watched their adult sons almost destroy their lives through drug use. Both mothers told stories of how skilled and gifted their respective sons were holding steady and good-paying positions before drugs became their sole reason for living. They talked of the businesses owned and then lost, homes forfeited to the bank, and wives and children cast aside. Each of their life plans came to nothing.

As we continued to discuss the challenge these moms face every day in trying to live hopeful, when the repercussions of sin have interrupted their sons' lives in the most dramatic possible ways, they admitted to sometimes struggling to keep their focus on Jesus and his promises to bring healing, hope, and redemption. These courageous women wanted nothing more than to please the Lord with their thoughts and their words. More than most, I believe these mothers fully hold onto gospel strength to live with daily hope, in spite of human weaknesses, by looking for the light (dim though it may be) one moment at a time. Two steps forward. Three steps backward. It's the dance step of life.

"May these words of my mouth and this meditation of my heart be pleasing in your sight, Lord, my Rock and my Redeemer." These words from Psalm 19:14 can become the model for which we aspire to live. When life interrupts our best-laid plans and our most earnest desires, we must make choices. As Paul Tripp notes, we are not just shaped by our experiences, but we also bring meaning and shape to them as well. Either of these two women could have viewed their situation in a different light. Instead of focusing on today's blessing of sobriety, they might have uttered words framed by worry or anger. Rather than living hopeful, these mothers could have chosen instead to despair, discouragement, and defeat.

But they didn't. They chose the better part.

Both of them did the hard work of looking to the Lord for his powerful provision amid their pain and suffering. Both women decided, one day at a time, to keep stepping into the future, confident that God will give them (and their families) the grace to continue. Neither of them leaves any room for bitterness or faultfinding or finger pointing. They don't have the energy to waste on such faithless responses. More often than not in this broken, battered world of hurting people, life's dance is a two-steps-forward-three-steps-backward dance. But as one mom said, "I just keep taking the next step."

## Take-away Action Thought

When I am faced with the great interruptions in life that upset my plans and topple my dreams, I will go straight to Psalm 19:14 and pray for the Lord to search my heart and my mind so that I can be pleasing in his sight. I want to respond to any and all of life's interruptions by shaping these experiences in a way that puts the full weight of my confidence in God alone.

## My Heart's Cry to You, O Lord

Father, help me to view all of life's unwanted and unexpected interruptions from the perspective that nothing surprises you. Though I may be shocked and dismayed, you are not. Help me to reframe every interruption I face in life with faith, hope, and joy. Give me the divine wisdom I need to see these interruptions as opportunities to settle myself before you and meditate on your unchanging character. Truly, Lord, let the words of my mouth and the meditations of my heart be pleasing to you. Always and forever. Amen.

## Faith Steps

1. Interruptions will certainly come. When they do, retreat to a quiet place and read through Psalm 19:14 until you thoroughly grasp what it means to speak words of truth and think about what is pleasing to the Lord. As you spend time with the Lord, his supernatural grace will equip you to respond to these interruptions with hope, faith, and love.

2. During the week, take a few minutes every day to jot down your greatest struggle in accepting and working through your current interruption, whatever it may be. Locate specific Bible promises to counteract any kind of worry anxiety you may be feeling.

3. Contact at least two friends and share your desire to respond to your life interruption with faith, peace, and hope. Ask them to check you on your words and attitude if you begin to worry again!

# Chapter 13

## Adjusting Relational Expectations for Good

You, my brothers and sisters, were called to be free. But
do not use your freedom to indulge the flesh; rather,
serve one another humbly in love. For the entire law
is fulfilled in keeping this one command: "Love your
neighbor as yourself." If you bite and devour each other,
watch out or you will be destroyed by each other.

Galatians 5:13–15

*Winning the war of words involves choosing our words
carefully. It is not just about words we say, but also about
the words we choose not to say. Winning the war is about
being prepared to say the right thing at the right moment,
exercising self-control. It is refusing to let our talk be
driven by passion and personal desire but communicating
instead with God's purposes in view. It is exercising the faith
necessary to be part of what God is doing at that moment.*

*Paul David Tripp*

Friends are the family we choose. How true. As I sat among
a group of women sharing their most pressing prayer requests for the coming week, I noticed a familiar theme.

Each of them asked for prayer for dealing kindly and lovingly with a relative with whom they found it difficult to communicate. I then realized that virtually everyone (at least everyone I know!) has that "someone" who challenges them in more ways than one.

For one woman, her "someone" was her mom, who just never has a positive comment about anything. Another woman's "someone" is her mother-in-law, who has never accepted her son's marriage to my lovely friend. Still another woman's "someone" is her son, who even as an adult continues to take financial advantage of my friend and her husband's generosity. This "someone" list can go on and on and on. If we're honest, we all have a "someone" and God wants us to learn how to handle this prickly relationship with grace and love (by honoring our "someone" above ourselves).

As we made notes of our particular prayer requests for the week, the conversation took a turn toward the importance of adjusting our relational expectations for good. By this, I mean for the good of the relationship and for good (that is, for once and for all!). We'd like to think that as we grow older, we have learned how to get along with others in a way that exhibits humility, grace, and puts others' welfare above our own. That sentiment, while ever hopeful, is not realistic in our broken world. We cannot change others, hoping to conform them (or coerce them) into the people we believe they should become.

Instead, our first task is to take stock of our own attitudes and actions and then hold both up to the mirror of close examination against Christ's standard to "love your neighbor as yourself." Once we honestly assess where we fall short (and we all will), we can then ask God for creative ways to exhibit Jesus' love in the lives of those we find challenging to love. An effective and necessary shortcut toward accepting and loving our personal "someone" is to accept the truth that we cannot change this person—remembering that change is God's territory. What we can and must do is adjust our relational expectations for good by looking for ways to offer blessing, even when curses are likely to be found.

One of the hardest aspects of adjusting our relational expectations is to accept the truth that there may be relationship issues that are never resolved. While we can do our best to make amends, build a bridge of effective communication, and serve our "someone" in love, we may never experience the breakthrough we hope and pray will happen. At this disappointing juncture, we all have a choice to make. Will we continue to press through our discouragement over not seeing change, or will we give up?

Paul is direct in his commands to the Galatian church. He tells them to value their freedom as Christ followers, not to indulge themselves but to humbly serve others. He exhorts his fellow believers to "love your neighbor as yourself," which fulfills all the commands. Each of us has to cast a vision for our particular "someone" by seeing what God wants for that person in view of eternity. Our words need to reflect God's mission—which is to win their hearts—and our actions need to reflect Jesus' sacrifice on the cross. Rather than feeling continually disappointed, we need to turn our eyes from ourselves and look intently at what God is trying to accomplish in the moment-by-moment, day-by-day interactions. Think of revelation, redemption, and restoration, and cast off those unrealistic relational expectations for good. For the sake of the relationship—and once and for all.

## Take-away Action Thought

When I struggle with "someone's" words and actions, I will go directly to this passage in Galatians and remind myself that it is my Christian duty to love that person humbly (without exception) and to love my neighbor (my "someone") as myself.

## My Heart's Cry to You, O Lord

Father, I am having trouble with my "someone." Just when I believe that we have turned a positive relational corner, old hurts (and fresh new ones) rise to the surface. Help me to let go of any expectations to which I may be clinging that hinder me from loving this person well. Give me the wisdom to know how to communicate in a way that is both loving and productive. I need your insight, Lord, to help me navigate this difficult relationship in such a way that I don't get bogged down by my own unrealistic expectations. Give me the eternal vision of what you want to do in this person's life, and help me to be constant in my love for them. Amen.

## Faith Steps

1. During the coming week, spend time alone with God asking him to reveal any unrealistic relational expectations you may be embracing of someone. If God shows you that you have been doing this, then confess and determine to move forward in a healthier, selfless way.

69

2. Meditate on the verses found in Galatians 5:13–15. Think deeply about what it looks like in real-life relationships to put others' welfare before your own. Again, if you need to confess before the Lord, do so and ask him to make you more sensitive to your motives as they relate to your relationships.

3. Write down a list of the people in your life with whom you are closest. Then, name by name, pray through this list, asking the Lord to help you see each person in light of eternity. Finally, jot down ways you can demonstrate genuine love toward each person in the coming weeks.

# Chapter 14

## It's Always Something (and That's a Good Thing)

"Because he loves me," says the LORD, "I will rescue
him; I will protect him, for he acknowledges my name.
He will call on me, and I will answer him; I will be with
him in trouble, I will deliver him and honor him. With
long life I will satisfy him and show him my salvation."

Psalm 91:14–16

*Worry is focused inward. It prefers self-protection over
trust. It can hear many encouraging words—even God's
words—and stay unmoved. It can be life dominating. It is
connected to your money and desires in that it reveals the
things that are valuable to you. It can reveal that you love
something more than Jesus. It crowds Jesus out of your life.*

*Edward Welch*

Whenever someone says "It's always something,"
we automatically assume something dreadful has
happened. You know it's true. A friend or a colleague will be chatting away and then suddenly those ominous
words seem to flow effortlessly from her lips and we inhale.

Waiting. Holding our breath for the details of something gone wrong. Let's be honest, for the majority of us this statement isn't often paired with a celebratory remark.

Imagine with me that instead of expecting bad news, we inhale, awaiting something lovely, something wonderful, something terrific. How would that positive anticipation change a situation or even change us? It can happen, you know. Rather than sitting around tallying up a burdensome number of sad stories, disappointing news, or troubling accounts, why not focus on the good?

Consider this real-life account of turning the tables on everything that can possibly go wrong with a person's health. Where do we find the more desperate and dire cases? In hospitals, of course. From the tiniest and frailest among us to the oldest, those who inhabit medical facilities remind us that every single breath we breathe is a gift. Life is precious. For good reason, hospitals frequently are the most feared places on earth. No one wants to be reminded of the frailty of life. And yet one particularly in-tune, savvy hospital recognized what their patients (families and staff) need most aren't miracle cures. What they need (and what we all need) are hopeful reminders that, yes, hard things happen in this life, but beauty arises just the same.

This particular hospital made it a policy to play a baby's lullaby over their speaker system every time a child was born on there. Imagine the impact a simple child's song has on everyone (patient, visitor, or staff) whenever this gentle tune plays. Multiple times a day every person within earshot hears a powerful reminder that new life prevails. The hopeless regain their will to live. The grieving pause to celebrate with another's joy. Those harboring dark thoughts suddenly change tracks. The weakened in body are reminded that a new life with all its possibilities has been born.

We are the ones who get to choose what our thoughts linger on, so let's get busy focusing on developing our gratefulness antennas. Let us begin and end each day counting up our blessings by following the Philippians 4:13 rule to think about whatever is "true, noble, right, pure, lovely, admirable, excellent, and praiseworthy." Once we start giving our thanks out loud, we'll find ourselves saying (and meaning), "It's always something—and that's a good thing!"

Above and beyond all the blessings we can contemplate that God has done, we can likewise give thanks for all the dangers, toils, and snares from which we have been protected by God. Just as this verse in Psalm 91 promises, God will rescue and protect us. Why? Because we love him. He promises to answer us when we cry out to him. God will be with us in our troubles and will deliver us. And there's even a bonus: God promises that we can live a satisfying life and look forward to eternity spent with him. Yes, it's always something. And with the love of God within us and surrounding us, that's a very good thing indeed.

### *Take-away Action Thought*

I will not become worried or distracted by the number of "things" that happen in my life that pull my attention away from God's love for me. Instead, I will count my blessings. I will name them one by one and see what the Lord has done.

## My Heart's Cry to You, O Lord

Father, please help me to stay focused on you and on your constant love for me. I don't want danger, toil, or snare to crowd Jesus out of my life. Help me to know within the deepest recesses of my heart and soul that you will never fail me. Your word promises this time and again. Give me the stalwart faith to believe you will come through, even when all the circumstances around me scream the opposite. I know you are the God who reigns on high. I know this to be true. Amen.

## Faith Steps

1.  When you start to feel overwhelmed by the sheer number of "things" that seem to pile one on another—those troubles that keep you up at night—open your Bible and begin reading and meditating on every verse you can find that promises God's perfect provision. Don't stop until you know within the deepest recesses of your heart that God will take care of you.

2.  If you begin to overthink about problems you're facing and worry starts to take hold of your thinking, call several friends who you know will pray for you. Share my struggles with them and ask for their ongoing intercession on your behalf.

3.  When the "things" that trouble you begin to add up, make a list with two columns. In the first column, write down everything you're worrying about. Next to each entry, locate a Bible verse that silences that specific fear and write it out in full. Then review your lists several times a day and carry it with you wherever you go so that you have God's promises within reach at all times.

# Chapter 15

## God Gives Grace for Our Needs

I sought the LORD, and he answered me; he
delivered me from all my fears.

Psalm 34:4

*Sometimes we live, sometimes we die, but for Christians it
means life either way. So, I can't say this enough—we can
feel the sad feelings, but we don't have to feel the hopeless ones.
Christians don't have to fear death, because for Christians,
to die is gain. Our fragile, broken bodies die, but we can be
peaceful knowing that for us, to die is to finally fully live. How
amazing! We can take our troubles to God and He can rescue
us—maybe from the circumstance, but definitely from the fear.*

*Scarlet Hiltibidal*

Some years ago, I was driving along in my car, listening
to a pastor preach about suffering, loss, and everything
hard and bad in this broken world. I remember thinking, *Well, this is sure an encouraging message!*

Despite that, I kept listening. After speaking about biblical
methodology for facing struggles in this world (as Jesus said we
would), he ended with a profound statement: Whenever we face

hardship, difficulties (large and small), suffering, disappointments, discouragement, devastation (in any shape or form), and
we are tempted to allow our emotions to hold sway over God's
promises of provision, God promises us grace for that specific
need—*our* need. God gives us the grace and strength to meet
that need at that moment in time. His message was simple,
straightforward, and easy to grasp.

On the flip side—and this is what was life changing for
me—when someone we love faces hardship, difficulties (large
and small), suffering, disappointments, discouragement, devastation (in any shape or form), and we start feeling sad for
them, God doesn't give *us* the grace to meet *their* specific need.
He gives *them* grace. That is, we don't need the same grace to
endure what another is going through. God gives grace to the
sufferer specific to her need. God doesn't give me grace to face
my friend's cancer diagnosis; but he does give me the grace
to come alongside her and support her. He may also give me
the wisdom and love I need to help serve her needs—and the
words I need to petition heaven on her behalf.

I'm not quite sure why I had spent the better part of my
forty-plus years as a Christ follower not understanding this principle. The words of this pastor changed the way I approached
suffering (my own and others). It also altered the way I choose
to pray (for myself and others).

When we or someone we care about suffers, we need to
understand that those emotions are real and it is natural to
feel them. What separates us as Christians from others without
a relationship with Jesus is that, yes, we suffer and it hurts;
but we don't suffer hopelessly, because we know Jesus has

conquered death. As Scarlet Hiltibidal writes, "Sometimes we live, sometimes we die, but for Christians it means life either way. So, I can't say this enough—we can feel the sad feelings, but we don't have to feel the hopeless ones."

God's magnificent grace is so amazing that when crushing life sorrows hit us head-on and we know that we're not strong enough to handle the situation, we can be certain that God is enough to help us through it. He has already conquered death. It has no sting for the Christ follower. Everything in between life's first breath and its final exhale is found in the security of God's faithful hands.

Part of our misconceptions about pain and suffering is that we tend to take on our loved ones' suffering and imagine ourselves in their situations and wonder how we would fare. We can mistakenly feel fear and be overwhelmed by another's suffering, which can then paralyze us. God wants us to enter into another's suffering by loving, serving, praying, and supporting that person. God, however, doesn't want us to drown under the weight of someone else's trials. He wants us to trust him to support and strengthen that person with his supernatural grace, remembering that God gives grace to the person who needs it. Sometimes that will be us. Other times it will be our loved one. But always, God promises to supply everything we require. "My God will meet all your needs according to the riches of his glory in Christ Jesus" (Phil. 4:19).

## Take-away Action Thought

When I start to feel overwhelmed and afraid because someone I love is suffering, I will remind myself that God promises to give my loved one the grace and strength they need. Likewise, I will remind myself that I do not need the same kind of grace they need for their suffering; I need the grace to support and serve my friend. Likewise, when I am suffering, I will need God's grace to endure my time of trials well. And when I suffer, I know that God will supply all the grace I need in that moment.

## My Heart's Cry to You, O Lord

Father, I find it so difficult to watch those I love suffer. I tend to think about it, mull it over in my mind, and become overly distraught over another's suffering. I know that you have promised us grace for every need. Help me to remember this when I attempt to put myself in someone else's painful position and then despair because I don't think I could endure what they're going through. Help me focus on your timeless scriptural promises on grace. Remind me that you will give me the grace to face my suffering, just as you give grace to my loved ones in their suffering. Amen.

## Faith Steps

1. When you begin to feel downhearted because of a loved one's suffering, remind yourself that God promises to supply their every need. Then sit down and pray for

your loved one and look for practical ways to ease their suffering.

2. When you are faced with suffering of your own, write out Psalm 34:4, speak it out loud, and then memorize it. Throughout the day, repeat this truth aloud, contemplating its amazing promise. Although you may feel sad, you will not be hopeless.

3. Journal my thoughts and emotions as you seek to find ways to serve and uplift others as they journey through suffering. Stay alert to any tendency toward feeling despair on behalf of others. Instead, place the full weight of your trust in God and his promises to supply every need your loved one has.

# Chapter 16

## *Learning to Want What God Wants*

I cry out to God Most High, to God, who vindicates
me. He sends from heaven and saves me, rebuking
those who hotly pursue me—God sends forth his love
and his faithfulness. . . . My heart, O God, is steadfast,
my heart is steadfast; I will sing and make music.

Psalm 57:2–3, 7

*Without Christ not one step, with Him anywhere.*
*David Livingstone*

Some time ago, I sat with a close friend, discussing our
families in general and our elderly parents in particular. At the time, both of my parents were doing well, so
my contribution to the conversation was minimal at best. My
friend's folks, however, were not doing so well. As my friend
described her parents' need to go into a retirement home and
how hard it had been on her mom most especially, she lamented
not being closer to them in physical proximity. I listened as she
described her mother's grief at the thought of this major change
so late in her life. It has always been her hope to live in their
family home until she died. But with one unexpected illness

after another, it became a matter of safety first and foremost, and personal preference ran a distant second.

For her mother, then, came the lingering grief, the loss of independence, the dismantling of a home full to the brim with material possessions as well as treasured memories. My friend truly understood her mom's sorrow and entered into her suffering as a beloved daughter and fellow Christ follower. My friend wondered how her mother, who had always been a stalwart believer, would fare living in a separate wing of the retirement home from her husband. For the first time in their married life, she would be separated from her beloved husband, who now suffered from Alzheimer's and needed special care. My friend wondered if this separation might very well send her mother to an early death.

Silently, we sat contemplating the situation and commiserating on how challenging these kinds of life changes are to everyone involved. My friend then said, "I wish my parents could have lived out their lives in their own home, but it cannot be. So, I have to learn to want what God wants more than what I want." My friend and I looked at each other and nodded in agreement, letting that profound truth sink in.

"God sends forth his love and his faithfulness. My heart, O God, is steadfast, my heart is steadfast; I will sing and make music." If only each of us would respond to life's unwanted and most difficult life challenges with this robust confidence, as expressed here in Psalm 57. The price, I know, of a steadfast heart is a willingly surrendered one. On some days in some situations, I can easily offer up my will for God's. On other days in different situations, I cling all the more tightly to my own preferences and carefully laid plans.

One lesson I learned from the echoes of my friend's sage words—"I have to want what God wants more than what I want"—is that my willing surrender to God's plans for me always makes the change less painful. It is difficult enough to accept unwanted disruptions in life without attempting to resist God's will in the midst of it. I therefore pray my prayers of willing submission. I implore God to fill me with the wisdom, grace, and strength to step through life's next door. Most of all, I beg him to change my heart so that I can truly learn to "want what God wants more than what I want." Every day. Every time. Through every change. I won't move an inch without Jesus, but I'll walk with him everywhere! Or as David Livingstone put it, "Without Christ not one step, with Him anywhere."

## Take-away Action Thought

When I am faced with a troubling change and resist surrendering my will to God's, I will spend time in prayer, asking the Lord to soften my heart into a willingly obedient and trusting one. Next, I will ask him to shore me up from the inside out so that I can steadfastly praise him for this opportunity to trust him.

## My Heart's Cry to You, O Lord

Father, here I am again, crying out to you for the grace and strength to willingly accept this change in my life. I know that I need to surrender my will to yours. But I also know you understand that I am in the midst of grieving this change. Although it's not what I would have planned, I know that you know what is best for me. Help me to rest in your sovereign rule, and create in me a steadfast heart that gratefully sings your praises no matter what the circumstances look life in my life. Amen.

## Faith Steps

1. When you are faced with unwelcome and unwanted changes in your life, take your questions and concerns directly to the Lord. Don't give in to the temptation to grumble or worry. Instead, settle yourself down in the Lord's presence and ask him to calm your heart.

2. As changes confront you, spend time daily pouring over God's word for verses that speak of his wisdom and understanding. Write these verses down and carry them with you throughout the day, rereading their powerful truths whenever you start to worry.

3. Share your heart's struggles with good friends and ask them to pray for you. Ask them to keep you accountable in your attitude by making sure that you are seeking to submit to God's will and want what God wants more than what you want.

## Chapter 17

### What to Do When the Losses Add Up

Finally, brothers and sisters, whatever is true, whatever
is noble, whatever is right, whatever is pure, whatever
is lovely, whatever is admirable—if anything is
excellent or praiseworthy—think about such things.

Philippians 4:8

*We become what we think. Our thought life—not our
circumstances—determines whether we are content. Our
thought life—not our friends, husband, children, job,
or anything else—determines our contentment!*

Linda Dillow

**M**any (many!) years ago when I was twelve, a favorite aunt and her children (my favorite cous-
ins) came to stay at our home for a few weeks
while they were looking for a house to rent in our town. One
evening my aunt shared the gospel message with me, and I
immediately responded with, "Yes, I want to know Jesus as my
Savior and Lord." That brief but eternally meaningful conversation changed my life—literally forever and ever. I've often
thought back to that conversation with my aunt; and because

it occurred right before Christmas, the timing has stuck with me all these years.

That momentous decision and the fact that my parents always made the holidays special for my brother and me is why I believe I am so fond of the time between Thanksgiving and New Year's Day. Everything about the holiday season with its gift preparations, decorating traditions, family celebrations, tantalizing smells, and yummy tastes serve up a mighty powerful image in my memory banks.

It's amazing how swiftly my mood can lift whenever I linger in those happy memories. It also startles me how suddenly my mood can plummet when I linger in troubling life situations. This recent holiday season was no exception.

The day before Christmas, I was busy in the kitchen preparing food to take over to our extended family that evening. I was buzzing along ahead of schedule and looking forward to our church's afternoon Christmas Eve service that preceded our family's gathering. Within minutes of each other, I received two text messages that brought the unwelcome and sad news of one friend's passing and a grim cancer diagnosis for another.

I stood there in my kitchen, rooted in the same place where I was just moments ago celebrating everything bright and beautiful about Jesus' birth. Seconds later, I felt the tears well in my eyes as I considered the accompanying sorrow that would be part of our friends' Christmases, present and future, with this death and this frightening cancer battle.

It was at that collision of the bitter and the sweet that I had to make up my mind. I had to choose to concentrate my thoughts as Paul says in Philippians 4:8 to think about everything that is "true, noble, right, pure, lovely, admirable, excellent, and praiseworthy." I just had to. Or else, I would succumb to the sorrow of this most recent distressing news. I could not rely on memories of past wonderful Christmases to lift my spirits at this moment, nor could I deny the very real tragedy happening right now. What I could do, however, was to remind myself of what is true. I started by turning my gaze to selected Scripture verses that hang on my refrigerator door. One by one, I said each one out loud. Then, I reread them silently. Only after fortifying myself with these comforting promises from God's word was I able to turn my thoughts to all that is true, right, and good.

When life's losses add up to more sorrow than our hearts can handle, we have a choice to make. We can follow Philippians 4:8 and start thinking about all that is "true, noble, right, pure, lovely, admirable, excellent, and praiseworthy." Or we can lose ourselves in the grief of circumstances that are always vying for our mind's attention. I love Linda Dillow's quotation above: "We become what we think." I want to radiate faith, love, hope, and joy.

Whether we like it or not, life and faith are uphill battles. The more years we have behind us, the more scarred are the soles of our feet and the beats of our hearts. One way to keep these losses from stealing our joy is to make a list from Philippians 4:8 and then and meditate on God's goodness in each word. For example, following the word *lovely*, I wrote, *Today's sunrise, the wheat fields surrounding us, the deer that leaped out from the wooded brush, the sailboats skimming across the lake, the infectious smile of a granddaughter, the kind response from a caring friend.* To my mind, each of these is what I consider lovely.

By going through the words from Philippians like this, I felt my heart and emotions transformed, particularly as I considered that all of these are precious, hand-delivered, and designed

86

gifts from our loving Lord. As I meditated on "all that is lovely," I found it powerful enough to lift my spirits. Whether we like it or not, we are indeed what we think. Sure, we have to feel our feelings, but we also have to learn to turn our thoughts to all that is "true, noble, right, pure, lovely, admirable, excellent, and praiseworthy." In this way, we will be able to see through faith's eyes, which will transform life's losses into something redemptive.

### *Take-away Action Thought*

When life's losses begin to add up and I feel discouraged, I will take pen to paper and start listing all that is "true, noble, right, pure, lovely, admirable, excellent, and praiseworthy."

### *My Heart's Cry to You, O Lord*

Father, help me to receive bad news with the abiding grace you always provide. Scripture reminds me that it is essential to apply myself to thinking thoughts that will build my faith and my trust as I place the entirety of my hope in you alone. Although the losses do add up as the years go by, I can also grow more skilled at turning swiftly toward you and your faithfulness in every situation. Help me to be quick to ask for your help when I feel undone by devastating news. Help me to be swift to offer my thanks for your ever-increasing blessings in my life. Amen.

## Faith Steps

1. When you receive troubling news of any kind, turn your mind to evidences of God's faithfulness by listing the "true, noble, right, pure, lovely, admirable, excellent, and praiseworthy" aspects of your life.

2. Speak of God's enduring faithfulness in times of trouble to those near you who are suffering, reminding them of specific moments in their personal history when God provided exactly what they needed.

3. When you are tempted to complain or despair, spend time alone with the Lord, waiting on him to bring comfort to your soul before you share with others whatever news is troubling you.

# Chapter 18

## Choosing to Cling to God Instead

Consider it pure joy, my brothers and sisters, whenever
you face trials of many kinds, because you know that
the testing of your faith produces perseverance. Let
perseverance finish its work so that you may be
mature and complete, not lacking anything.

James 1:2–4

*In our suffering God is at work to give us something much
better than what we want. He's not content to dispense
temporary relief, when eternal change is what we really
need. In the zeal of redeeming love, he uses hard tools to
product soft but sturdy hearts, and that's a very good thing.*

*Paul David Tripp*

**W**hy is it that in the midst of the most effective
seasons of ministry and labor for the Lord, he
sometimes sidelines his children with debilitating sickness? I asked my friend this question and then sat
pondering this common phenomenon. She then recommended
a new book by Paul Tripp, one of my favorite authors, called
*Suffering: Gospel Hope When Life Doesn't Make Sense.* This book
was exactly what I needed.

In his opening chapters, Tripp recounts what he had anticipated would be a brief check-in at a local hospital for some minor symptoms he was experiencing. Within hours, he was admitted to the ICU with failing kidneys and a whole team of specialists working diligently to save his life. Naturally, his first response was shock and unbelief. What, he wondered, was happening here?

Next, Tripp describes what he terms "the spiritual battle of suffering" as the days turned to weeks, months, and then years of physically debilitating circumstances. Written several years after his initial life-changing diagnosis, Tripp's book is a compelling read as he can now unpack his terrifying experience and how it has forever changed him and his life.

One of the most important lessons Tripp learned was how deeply ingrained in each of us is that portion of stubborn independence and self-reliant pride that can surface during suffering but remains hidden at other times in our lives. He recognized how he had taken for granted the physical strength with which he enthusiastically served the Lord through weekend conferences, writing, and counseling. When he was suddenly and inexplicably sidelined because of his failing kidneys (and six subsequent surgeries), he realized how much he craved control in his life.

Throughout his journey back to semi-wellness (he will never be the same physically robust man he was prior to his illness), Tripp understands that the Lord will always make the best use of any type of suffering his children endure. God loves us enough to rescue us from our own delusions of strength so that we turn to him for everything we need to live. Rather than allow us to continue to falsely trust in our physical strength, good health, vocational achievements, illusions of control, or any number of "false idols" we cling to, God will allow whatever it takes to turn our hearts and minds toward him so that we are eternally changed. In short, Tripp writes, "[God] uses hard tools to produce soft but sturdy hearts, and that's a very good thing."

The apostle James tells us to consider it pure joy when we face trials, because we know that the end result will produce maturity and completeness within us—an eternal readiness. Of course, we know that suffering is hard. Tripp notes that suffering will strip us bare of everything we believed theologically and force us to rethink what we know about God and his promises. Suffering in any capacity is truly a long, difficult spiritual battle. We can, however, emerge on the other side of our travails more sturdily fitted to serve God and others as we are transformed from the inside out. Which of us wouldn't desire a "soft but sturdy heart" to serve others better? Which of us wouldn't long for comfort from another whose heart was also "soft but sturdy"?

One of Tripp's contemporaries, David Powlison—speaker, author, and biblical counselor—is suffering from pancreatic cancer. He recently spoke at a conference a friend of mine attended, saying, "My life is not a medical drama. Rather, my life is hidden in Christ." Powlison says that he will not allow himself to look beyond today and worry about what may occur tomorrow. Indeed, he reminds us that to do so is to sin. I'm in awe of his conviction and afraid that if I had to face the same grim diagnosis, I would not be strong enough to handle it in a similar peaceful way. And that is exactly the problem. I'm not strong enough. Tripp isn't strong enough. Powlison isn't strong enough. No one is strong enough.

Only when we allow God to strip away all that we cling to instead of him for our comfort and strength will we experience the peace that passes all understanding. Only when we allow him to search the deepest recesses of our hearts and minds will we discover and then cast out any "false idols" that have been hindering us. True enough, none of us wants to suffer. But suffering comes to all of us in one form or another. It therefore behooves us to learn what it means to suffer well before we are faced with some of the most difficult battles of our lives. I pray we all emerge from our seasons of suffering with "soft but sturdy hearts."

## *Take-away Action Thought*

When I am in the midst of a terrifying experience and uncertain what will happen, I will ask the Lord to strip away anything to which I am clinging for false comfort and strength that does not come from him.

## *My Heart's Cry to You, O Lord*

Father, I am in the midst of something that frightens me more than I can say. You already know what I'm feeling and how my first response is to try and regain come control over this terrifying situation. I confess that I am afraid and I find myself completely paralyzed by this fear. It's all I can think about during the day, and at night I lay awake with a pounding heart. Help me, Lord! I need your grace and your strength to cast all my care away from me and onto your faithful shoulders. It is you alone I trust to see me through this battle. Amen.

## Faith Steps

1. As a personal challenge, take some time this week to sit down with pen and paper and quietly wait on the Lord, asking him to show you where you struggle to relinquish control and where you cling to "false idols" rather than to God alone.

2. In response to what the Lord reveals to you about desiring to be in control or leaning on "false idols" for comfort and security, share these insights with a friend and ask them to help keep you accountable if they see you trying to control your life instead of trusting God to supply all you need.

3. Since you know how any type of suffering can become the "drama" of your life, memorize James 1:2–4 and daily exercise a grateful spirit to the Lord for the good you are confident he will accomplish within your heart.

# Chapter 19

## Developing Your "Prayer Walk" (Literally or Figuratively)

Love the LORD your God with all your heart and with all your
soul and with all your strength. These commandments that
I give you today are to be on your hearts. Impress them on
your children. Talk about them when you walk along the road,
when you lie down and when you get up. Tie them as symbols
on your hands and bind them on your foreheads. Write
them on the doorframes of your houses and on your gates.

Deuteronomy 6:5–9

*The gospel of Jesus and the promises of God in the word
of God work right now. Every one we read reminds us
this is not the end. It cannot be the end. The promises
are tied to God and He can have no end. Every promise
that melts our heart and shapes how we see our world
and our own self gives us strength to carry on and do
what God has put us here to do—love the other scared
people in this broken world. We have promises.*

Scarlet Hiltibidal

*D*id you know you talk to yourself?" The first time I heard those words, I was quite surprised. My oldest daughter then told me how when she was upstairs in her bedroom studying, she often heard me downstairs in the kitchen—talking to myself. Good grief! At first, she assumed I was on the phone, until one day she came down the stairs and saw me working at the kitchen counter and—you guessed it—talking to myself! As I said, her statement really threw me.

Some folks I know are verbal processors, but I'm not one of them. I tend to think silently through problems, turning them over in my mind before I begin speaking—which is why my daughter's remark caught me off guard. My first response to her was, "What have I been saying?" She laughed and explained that she couldn't hear what I was saying, just that I was talking. So with this new tidbit of information about myself, I began paying more attention to my thoughts and my words. This may also explain why I find comfort walking along the lakeshore whenever weather permits. In this way, I could talk (knowingly or not) out loud so that only the Lord would hear me!

I'm often reminded of the importance of thinking before speaking—specifically, considering the amazing and eternal promises of God out loud and often (to myself and to others). I've always agreed with Paul Tripp's assertion that we are the most important and influential voice in our lives, because we talk to ourselves from morning until night. Thus what we tell ourselves (silently or out loud) can literally (or figuratively) make or break us. This is why I try daily to honor what God says about impressing his commandments "your children. Talk about them when you walk along the road, when you lie down and when you get up. Tie them as symbols on your hands and bind them on your foreheads. Write them on the doorframes of your houses and on your gates."

So how are you at processing the hardships found in this broken world? Do you, like me, sometimes get bogged down with the overwhelming number of heavy news flashes you receive daily? Does it sometimes feel as though God is far off and allowing way too much in the way of disaster, death, and destruction on planet Earth? How, then, do we counteract this onslaught of unwanted suffering, pain, and sorrow? We begin by talking to God in prayer. Whether we choose to get down on our knees in a private space and silently cry out to our heavenly Father, or take a walk outdoors, what's important is to begin a conversation with him. The spiritual discipline of developing a daily "prayer walk" (whether it's pacing around your kitchen or setting paces on a track field, or just sitting in an armchair) is key to keeping your head above the waves that threaten to wash over you.

Today and every day, the most important priority we have as Christians is to carve out some alone time with God. We are free, of course, to choose the time and the place. What's vital is that we choose to make spending time in his word and in prayer as essential to our daily lives as drinking, eating, and sleeping. Only when we rightly position our time spent with God will the remainder of our minutes, hours, and days become all that we hope they can be. We need God's daily infusion of truth, hope, grace, and light to equip us to go out into the world and love the broken people he sends our way.

## Take-away Action Thought

When I feel overwhelmed by the pressures of the day and grief over the world's sufferings discourages me, I will silence the doubtful voices in my head. I will break away and spend time alone in God's presence, talking to him and allowing him to minister to my weary soul.

## My Heart's Cry to You, O Lord

Father, too many demands and worries have filled these past weeks for me, and I am completely exhausted. I feel emotionally drained by the bad news I receive from every quarter. My family, my friends, my church circle, neighbors, and even acquaintances all seem to be carrying such heavy loads of one sort or another. I need you to revive my heart and remind me of your constant love and care for all of us. Help me to set aside time every single day to be spent in solitude with you. I need your heavenly perspective on this world's brokenness, so that I have the passion and the strength to carry on loving other scared and hurting people. Amen.

## Faith Steps

1. As you plan out your week, look over my calendar and block out daily time to spend alone with God. Make this a priority and forfeit other optional activities so that you have both time and energy to give your full attention to the Lord.

2. If you do not already have a consistent prayer walk in place, develop one that works best for you. Using a calendar, keep track of each day you keep this commitment and journal how those prayer walks, whether literally or figuratively, made a difference in your day.

3. Write out the passage above from Deuteronomy and carry it with you. Then each day of the week, institute a different aspect of this command. At the end of the week, review how obeying these directives changed you and equipped you to better love those you are called to serve.

# Chapter 20

## Leaning into Jesus for the Strength You Need

God chose the foolish things of the world to shame the wise; God chose the weak things of the world to shame the strong. God chose the lowly things of this world and the despised things—and the things that are not—to nullify the things that are, so that no one may boast before him. It is because of him that you are in Christ Jesus, who has become for us wisdom from God—that is, our righteousness, holiness, and redemption.

1 Corinthians 1:27–30

*One of the hardships of suffering is profound feelings of weakness and inability. Suffering powerfully exposes our humanness. It reminds us that we are weak, small, and lacking in power and how limited in resources we really are. Suffering doesn't make us weak; it simply exposes the weaknesses that have been there all along. It exposes the delusion of our sovereignty and independent capability. It's painful to be confronted with who we really are and how needy and dependent we are.*

*Paul David Tripp*

Joyous Faith

*T*his past week, I have been under a literal vortex of wind, snow, ice, and crazy subzero temperatures. Schools closed. Businesses shut down. Government buildings closed. Highways and byways were cordoned off. Even our electric company that supplies most of the lower half of our state's electricity cautioned everyone to turn down their thermometers because of a fire in one of its main power stations. From the pictures I saw on social media, it looked like the entire state of Michigan was closed. It was crazy and even a little scary.

No one who lives in our state is a stranger to the dangers of Michigan's ever-shifting inclement weather patterns. From tornado warnings in the summer to brutal ice storms in the winter, Michiganders are prepared—as prepared, that is, as anyone can be in this uncertain world. The truth is that no matter how diligently we prepare for the worst-case scenarios, there's much that remains beyond our control.

It's those beyond-our-control scenarios that keep me checking and rechecking my available resources. I tapped my phone app for local weather every ten minutes or so on those especially arctic chill days so I could plan my day accordingly. It's not just our plans that get squashed by the uncertain; we also get a little uptight making sure we have the necessities in place. Food. Water. Heat. A car that will get through anything. An extra battery or two for said vehicle. A whole house generator and plenty of fuel for days of backup. As I said, it was crazy and even a little scary.

When we forget that we were born in need and will pass into the next life in the same way, we can become fearful or stressed. When we, however, realize that something scary is outside our ability to control (fix, heal, transform, redeem), this is when God can move in. Weakness isn't when bad things happen around me (or inside of me). True weakness—the crazy, scary kind—is when I believe it's all up to me to handle whatever is threatening me, even when it's the wickedest storm to hit Michigan in years.

"It is because of him that you are in Christ Jesus, who has become for us wisdom from God—that is, our righteousness, holiness, and redemption." This passage from 1 Corinthians should awaken us to the breadth and depth of Christ's complete work within us. It's never been about our strength, abilities, giftedness, accomplishments, or successes. Instead, it's about recognizing that the most dangerous part about being weak is our inability to admit it and then turn to Jesus for what we need. If we can clearly identify our weakness in our sufferings or hardships, then we can allow this fact to force us to lean all the more deeply into the loving arms of our strong Savior.

How about you? Have you been trying to stay strong in the face of something so hard, so awful, that you have forgotten that the perfect love of Jesus stands ready to rescue you from your false self-help status? The truth is that none of us can save ourselves from anything in our own strength. The good news, however, is that Jesus has already finished his completed work on the cross (on our behalf) and now we can lay claim to our godly inheritance of righteousness, holiness, and redemption. Now that is something to boast about—that Jesus' perfect work will continue to transform us from the inside out until that perfect day. Yes, sometimes it does feel scary to understand how very weak we all are, how dependent each of us is on God for every breath we take. But in reality, it's a scary, good thing.

## Take-away Action Thought

When I start to feel overwhelmed by something that scares me because I realize I am not in control, I will lean in all the more to Jesus' perfect love, confident that he is able to meet my every need. I will thank him for my weakness, knowing that when I am weak, Jesus' power rests upon me.

## My Heart's Cry to You, O Lord

Father, lately things have been pressing in on me in such a rapid pace that I feel overwhelmed and weary at the thought of having to handle these unexpected difficulties. In my heart, I know that your love is constant and your care for me is personal. But sometimes, I mistakenly get sidetracked by the lie that I have to be strong and in control of everything that happens in my life. This is absurd, and yet I fall into this trap time and again. Help me, Lord, to lean all the harder into your loving arms when I begin to feel panicky or anxious about things that are out of my control. Keep me focused on you alone. Amen.

## Faith Steps

1. Write out the passage above from 1 Corinthians and spend time unpacking each statement as you prayerfully ask God to help you understand how comforting and powerful this truth is to you personally. Note any specific fears or personal weaknesses you have and then pray through these verses until you truly grasp their truths.

2. Make a specific list of everything you fear in life. Then describe how you usually cope with them. Next, share these findings with a good friend and talk through each scenario, creating a biblical plan of action for the coming days.

3. Prayerfully ask the Lord to reveal to you ways in which you hinder his good and perfect work in your life by trying to be self-sufficient. Then look for ways to invest yourself in the lives of others, realizing how interdependent you are on them (as they are on you). As you serve them, humbly allow fellow believers to also be a blessing with their service toward you.

# Chapter 21

## Joyous Laughter: A Key to Aging with Resilience

He has made everything beautiful in its time. He
has also set eternity in the human heart; yet no one
can fathom what God has done from beginning to
end. I know that there is nothing better for people
than to be happy and to do good while they live.

Ecclesiastes 3:11–12

*You will never be completely happy on earth simply
because you were not made for earth. Oh, you will have
moments of joy. You will catch glimpses of light. You will
know moments or even days of peace. But they simply
do not compare with the happiness that lies ahead.*

*Max Lucado*

Aging is merciless, but Jesus is full of mercy. A friend
shared that insightful truth with me some months
ago, and I haven't forgotten it. This morning, in fact,
sitting around our kitchen table with three other couples with
whom Jim and I meet monthly, I was reminded the truth of this
yet again. After we consumed a hearty breakfast, shared some

laughs, and caught up on personal business, we watched a short teaching video and then discussed it. We tossed around thoughts and ideas and shared personal stories. Oh, and we laughed. We laughed a lot.

It's in those brief two hours on a Saturday morning once a month that I witness the beautiful intersection of the human and the divine. We, of course, make up the human components that eat, drink, talk, share, and laugh. God, through his word and prayer, makes up the divine as he guides our conversation and we offer up our thanks and our requests. I often reflect on our time together as one of the highlights of my month, because we're all facing the same battles for the most part, and we all find ourselves nodding in agreement as we each talk about life's challenges. Specifically, as we are all getting older, the statement that aging is indeed merciless but Jesus is full of mercy applies so well to our situations.

Once we've finished working through our discussion questions, we share our prayer requests—and this is when I'm reminded how tough life can be. As I jot down everyone's prayer requests and compile them for the group, I'm continually aware that for believers the best is yet to come. Certainly, there is no shortcut through suffering in the now; but in the long tomorrow, nothing will compare to what lies ahead. And that's a promise that should fill us with joyous laughter.

I always appreciate how Max Lucado describes these moments when all seems right in the world. You know the feeling: when the meal is as satisfying as the company you share it with and the conversation and laughter come easily. It's in those moments when I "catch glimpses of light," as Lucado terms it, and I can imagine what heaven will be like. That beautiful intersection of all that is right and beautiful and good. Enjoying every aspect of an experience in the way God intended it before the Fall.

These transcendent moments may not happen often; but when they do, it's as though we're uplifted from the inside out and momentarily even our aging-is-merciless complaints are silenced. I'm a firm believer in the healing power of laughter, and laughing with people who know and love you is all the better. Again, Lucado describes it so succinctly,

You will never be completely happy on earth simply because you were not made for earth. Oh, you will have moments of joy. You will catch glimpses of light. You will know moments or even days of peace. But they simply do not compare with the happiness that lies ahead.

He is absolutely correct. We were not made for earth. We were made for so much more, and I am grateful when God blesses me with these reminders of what's yet to come.

## Take-away Action Thought

When I feel low because the challenges of aging are catching up with me, I will surround myself with friends and family who make me laugh. I will intentionally spend time with those who smile easily, who are upbeat, and who know how to laugh even through the hard times in life.

## My Heart's Cry to You, O Lord

Father, there are days when I feel my age deeply. I feel slower and less energetic. I sleep less soundly and then have to battle against responding irritably during the day. Help me to accept that fact that my body is growing older and will slow down. Parts of my physical being will eventually stop functioning altogether, but that doesn't mean my inner self has to despair. Give me the wisdom to keep my eyes trained on the long tomorrow and the promise of heaven. And give me the wisdom to laugh, often. Surround me with friends and family who have learned the healing power of laughter, even through the darkest days. Amen.

## Faith Steps

1. Each day this week, build laughter into your life. Whether you watch a funny movie, read a lighthearted book, or listen to a comedian, make it a priority to laugh more.

2. Invite family and friends over for a game night for an evening of fun. Play games, tell stories, and simply enjoy a relaxing time together.

3. Spend time journaling about specific memories when you laughed and enjoyed yourself. Then make plans to repeat some of these activities in the coming weeks and months.

# Chapter 22

## Embracing Forgiveness, Even When It Costs You

"Our Father in heaven,
hallowed by your name,
your kingdom come,
your will be done,
on earth as it is in heaven.
Give us today our daily bread.
And forgive us our debts,
as we also have forgiven our debtors.
And lead us not into temptation,
but deliver us from the evil one."

Matthew 6:9–13

*The Lord's Prayer commands us to pray, "Forgive us our debts as we forgive our debtors," right after it instructs us to pray for daily bread. Practicing forgiveness is something we must do daily in the same way we ask for the daily provision of food. It is a part of everyday life, not something for life's "big" sins and events.*

Tim Lane and Paul Tripp

*A* few weeks ago, I overheard a heated one-sided phone conversation while waiting for the hospital elevator door to open. I had just pressed the down button on the ICU floor elevator and was silently giving thanks that my mother's surgery had gone so well earlier in the afternoon. As I waited for the elevator to stop on my floor, I couldn't help but hear this distraught middle-aged man talking loudly into his phone. He kept repeating, "I never expected my own sister to betray me like this . . . at a time like this . . . I never expected it."

I have no idea to whom this emotionally charged man was talking; but as I continued to wait for the elevator, I heard the desperation in his voice as he told the listener how angry he was at his sister. Given the fact we were on the ICU floor and he was a visitor, I'm fairly certain someone he loved was there as a patient. The more this man talked, the more upset he became. I felt for him, even though I had no idea what the facts were surrounding this problem between him and his sister.

I did realize, however, that unless they worked it out (and soon), whomever they both loved who was fighting for their life in the ICU unit was going to be facing not only a long arduous physical recovery but would likely be embroiled in their family squabble. It hurt just to think about how much mental, emotional, and physical energy we deplete by relational impasses. Clearly, this man was going to have to make some serious decisions in the coming days. Would he make the attempt to communicate with his sister or not? Would he have the courage to sit down and engage in a respectful conversation with her? Would he forgive her for whatever she had done? I could only hope he would. I finally got on my elevator, pressed the main lobby button, and prayed for him to make the choice to fully forgive.

Over the next few days, I gave that conversation some serious thought. I've also tried to faithfully pray for this man and his situation. I tried to put myself in his position and consider how difficult it must be to have a loved one in the ICU and be simultaneously embroiled in a family dispute. Would I be quick to forgive? Or would I attempt to put the disagreement out of my mind and try to focus solely on my loved one's health? I hope I would have the wisdom and courage to do both.

Each of us has endured heartrending experiences with others (family, friends, colleagues, neighbors, fellow believers) when we believe we have been wronged and we have a choice to make. Do we forgive or not? Do we obey Jesus' instruction to pray "Forgive us our debts, as we also have forgiven our debtors," or do we disobey? None of us can make the claim that we have not sinned against another. But do we take our own sins against others as seriously as when we feel wronged by someone?

Consider these thoughtful comments by C. S. Lewis on forgiveness in *The Weight of Glory*:

> To forgive the incessant provocations of daily life—to keep on forgiving the bossy mother-in-law, the bullying husband, the nagging wife, the selfish daughter, the deceitful son—how can we do it? Only, I think, by remembering where we stand, by meaning our words when we say in our prayers each night, "Forgive us our trespasses as we forgive those that trespass against us." We are offered forgiveness on no other terms. To refuse is to refuse God's mercy for ourselves. There is no hint of exceptions and God means what he says.

## Take-away Action Thought

When I am faced with a hurtful situation, I will to choose to obey Jesus in Matthew 6 to forgive the offense against me. I will not make excuses for holding onto anger so that it develops into bitterness and resentment. If I find it difficult to forgive, I will speak with a godly friend or mentor and ask them to help me work biblically through the process of forgiveness.

## My Heart's Cry to You, O Lord

Father, I am in a hard and emotionally charged situation where I am struggling to overcome hurt and betrayal from someone I care about. This is especially difficult, because I didn't see this coming and I feel blindsided by their words and their actions. Help me to focus on the great sacrifice Jesus made for me on the cross when he died for my sins. This amazing act of unconditional love is so powerful that I am compelled to forgive others when they sin against me. Shore me up with your love and grace, and give me everything I need to surrender this situation to you and obey you as I choose to forgive. Amen.

## Faith Steps

1. Spend time reading and rereading Scripture passages that talk about forgiveness. Remind yourself of Christ's great sacrifice on the cross as he died to pardon you of all your sins. Ask the Lord to give you the desire and the grace to fully forgive.

2. This week, spend time every day in prayer, asking the Lord to reveal to your heart anyone you have not forgiven. If God shows you that you have not forgiven (or that you need to seek forgiveness), choose to forgive immediately and wipe the slate clean or make reparations as needed with others.

3. If you are tempted to keep bringing up an offense in your mind, turn your thoughts to the Lord's Prayer and say the verses out loud. Then ask the Lord (and others you trust) to keep you accountable in seeking full forgiveness and granting it.

# Chapter 23

## Becoming an Instrument of Reconciliation

Let your gentleness be evident to all. The Lord is
near. Do not be anxious about anything, but in every
situation, by prayer and petition, with thanksgiving,
present your requests to God. And the peace of
God, which transcends all understanding, will
guard your hearts and minds in Christ Jesus.

Philippians 4:5–7

*It is not good enough to communicate so that you*
*can be understood. You should communicate so*
*clearly that you cannot be misunderstood.*

Ken Sande

Many of my friends are instruments of reconciliation; and the more years that go by, the more swiftly each of these friends senses the urgency to make things right before it's too late. While I could share story after story where these individuals have sought out others, be it family or friends, and made the courageous attempt to bring peace where there was strife, one story holds the most weight for me.

Day after day, this particular friend visited the nursing home where her father was slowly dying from a combination of numerous physical ailments and diseases. She would sit quietly next to his bed with the hope he would wake up while she was there. Day by day, week after week, my friend took the time to visit and silently pray for her father. As she sat interceding for his soul, she told me that in those lonely quiet moments, her mind would sometimes replay her father's harsh words (that is, when he bothered to speak to her at all). She would painfully recall how he seemed to prefer her brothers' presence over her own. My friend also shuddered as she remembered the night he came into her bedroom late at night and she fought him off.

As a believer in Christ, my friend understood as an adult that her father had endured an abusive childhood himself, and she realized that much of what he said and had done erupted from an angry, embittered heart. She had long ago forgiven him for his sins against her. The evidence for this supernatural forgiveness was played out by her selfless care for him as an elderly and infirm aged adult. Over the years, she had tried sharing her faith with her father, but he always turned away from her in silence.

She never gave up, and the eventual fruit of her persistent faith came just a few days before her father's death. After years of pleading for his soul at the throne at God, my friend's father gave his life to Christ. He asked for forgiveness and became reconciled with God. My friend had lovingly kept her eyes on the eternal, even when her heart struggled to pray for the man who had caused her so much pain in her life. Through her desire to be reconciled horizontally with her earthly father, he was eventually reconciled vertically with his heavenly Father.

I wonder how often the Holy Spirit gently nudges me to go and initiate a conversation with someone and I shush him? If I'm honest, it probably happens more frequently than I care to admit. I'd love to believe that I continually walk in step with the Spirit, but I know better. Too frequently, I'm distracted because I'm busy or I'm too busy noticing someone else's failure to love me well. In my shortsighted sinfulness, I forget the eternal. I need to do better.

I want to emulate my friend's example by intentionally seeking to reconcile others to God by being a peacemaker in word and deed. I need to let go of minor offenses and deal seriously with large ones. My words need to be laced with gentleness, always speaking with the intent to work through strife, so that there is healing and forgiveness between me and others. My prayers need to be full of faith and expectant that God can work a relational miracle of sorts. My words need to clearly convey that above all else, my most earnest hope and desire is for my friend to know the saving love of Jesus Christ. Our horizontal reconciliation is my temporal desire, but the eternal vertical reconciliation is my ultimate aim.

*Take-away Action Thought*

I will ask the Lord to reveal to me any person with whom I need to seek reconciliation and then prayerfully prepare to meet with that person. I will also seek out several close friends to pray along with me before, during, and after my conversation.

## My Heart's Cry to You, O Lord

Father, I've been putting off a conversation with someone with whom I've had a falling out. If it were up to me, I would probably avoid this person for the rest of my life. It's painful for me to even bring to mind what passed between us. Help me, Lord, to fully forgive and to seek forgiveness for any part I had in this breach in our relationship. Show me how to pray before I enter into a conversation, and help me prepare as best as I can before we meet to talk. Give me your divine wisdom to choose my words carefully and to have as my ultimate aim both horizontal and vertical reconciliation. Amen.

## Faith Steps

1. First, spend time with your Bible, pen, and paper in hand, and prayerfully seek to recognize if you have anyone in your life with whom you need to seek reconciliation and restoration. If God reveals anyone to you, then begin praying how to best enter into a conversation with this individual.

2. After you have given enough time and thought as to how to best approach this person, write out what you specifically need to discuss. Make a list of the important details, and rehearse your words in order to prepare as best as you can.

3. If this person is willing to meet with you, ask several friends to pray before, during, and after your conversation. Keep in the forefront of your heart and mind the hope for reconciliation (both horizontally between you and vertically with God).

# Chapter 24

## Cultivating Contentment

Rejoice always, pray continually, give thanks in all
circumstances, for this is God's will for you in Christ Jesus.
1 Thessalonians 5:16–18

*Tell Him you're going to offer up to Him every situation
and circumstance in your life, even the ones that are still
sensitive to the touch, the ones that make absolutely no
sense, the ones you just really don't understand why you're
having to put up with right now. No matter how hard
it gets, no matter what someone says to you, no matter
how long it goes on or where it might lead, you will drop
the full weight of it at His feet every night, be thankful
for His strength that brought you through the day, and
wait for His mercies that will be new in the morning (even
though you may start needing them again at 12:01!)*

*Nancy Leigh DeMoss*

You never know how people are going to react when
you ask them, "How are you?" I can attest, however, to the fact that I could accurately predict the
response of one particular elderly lady. It didn't matter what

was happening in her life or outside in the world. She always responded with the sincerest, "I'm just so blessed. God has been so good to me." While most folks who speak these saccharine-sounding words so often overused in Christian circles might draw a raised eyebrow or two, this dear woman of God meant every one.

It didn't matter that I was privately aware that her circumstances weren't anything to cheer about. Her health was failing and she sorely missed her deceased husband. Plus her beloved companion cat had just died and her best friend had recently moved to another state. This precious woman was in her mid-eighties, and she always responded with a smile on her lips and cheering words. She was a wonder to behold.

I remember sitting around a table with ten or so women of all ages. Whenever this elderly lady began to speak, silence immediately reigned in the room. Why? Because we all wanted some portion of her sweet spirit and hard-earned wisdom to take possession of our hearts and minds through osmosis. As she spoke, something pretty amazing would happen. She would share about a personal hardship she had experienced and how painful it had been to accept initially. Then, without fail, she would say, "But God has been so good to me." Then she would tell us how God had ministered to her broken heart and drawn her close to his heart of love through the painful process. Oh how I long to be that woman when I am in my eighties. Truth be told, I want to be that woman today!

Gratitude is a hard-won spiritual attitude and discipline that all of us can learn to exercise in our lives. While my dear friend told us of her trials through the years and how God graciously met her every need, what stuck with me the most was when she determined that choosing gratitude had to be a daily (sometimes hourly) decision. A decision that she made every single day, sometimes multiple times a day, to offer up praise and thanksgiving to the Lord no matter what her challenges looked like—or how long they might last.

In her younger years, her husband traveled frequently for business, leaving her home alone for weeks at a time with their children. He also transplanted their family numerous times through the years whenever his job required him to do so. My friend is an introvert and every move cost her something relationally. She struggled making new friends and often experienced loneliness, and yet she learned to "rejoice always, pray continually, give thanks in all circumstances, for this is God's will for [her] in Christ Jesus." She learned the secret of living a contented, grateful, happy life by continually surrendering her desires to the Lord. I'll say it again: I want to be like that in my eighties and even today!

## Take-away Action Thought

When I start to feel discontented with something happening in my life, I will squelch the desire to grumble. Instead, I will begin praising the Lord for who he is—my unchanging, faithful, sovereign heavenly Father who loves me and only wants what is best for me.

## My Heart's Cry to You, O Lord

Father, I struggle with the sin of grumbling. I always believe I know what is best for me and my family. Help me to cease this ungodly striving to be in control and willingly surrender my will for yours. I need to be fully confident, no matter how circumstances may appear, that you want only the very best for me. Fortify my faith so I can honor you even when I'm disappointed, confused, or feeling defeated. Please give me your grace and the strength of will to give you thanks in all circumstances, because it is your will for me to go through these difficulties. Open my eyes to the blessings all around me. Amen.

## Faith Steps

1. Rejoice always, pray continually and give thanks in all circumstances, for this is God's will for you in Christ Jesus. Write down these three steps: rejoice, pray, and give thanks. Seek to honor the Lord every day through this three-step process.

2. Offer up to God whatever situation you are in that is difficult for you right now. Journal your thoughts, emotions, and past reactions to challenging circumstances. Then write out a new and better action plan, beginning with a time of praise and thanksgiving to the Lord every morning.

3. If you continue to struggle with hard situations unfolding in your life, come before the Lord and ask him to give you the strength and the grace to relinquish control completely to him.

# Chapter 25

## Creating Beautiful Spaces in This Temporary Place

Let us hold unswervingly to the hope we profess, for he who promised is faithful. And let us consider how we may spur one another on toward love and good deeds, not giving up meeting together, as some are in the habit of doing, but encouraging one another—and all the more as you see the Day approaching.

Hebrews 10:23–25

*When you take food to the poor, that's an act of worship. When you give a word of kindness to someone who needs it, that's an act of worship. When you write someone a letter to encourage them or sit down and open your Bible with someone to teach them, that's an act of worship.*

*Max Lucado*

Many years ago, a friend gave me a copy of *Five Aspects of Womanhood: A Biblical Theology Femininity* by Barbara K. Mouser, which focuses on the repercussions of sin on our physical world. The once perfect and peace-full planet that Adam and Eve governed together by communing with God was utterly destroyed. From that time until Jesus returns, everything on earth is now temporary. Although I understood this concept intellectually, I had never connected this specific statement to the angst I felt as a young wife and mom, who was working hard to create a beautiful space for my family. Reading this book and then contemplating its truth gave me pause, and eventually a great deal of comfort. It's true: everything as we know it is temporary; and as such, we need to provide constant care and creative rebuilding.

Does the scope of this truth hit you? I recall rereading it until I understood what the author is trying to communicate. She is telling us Christians that, although we can give it our best effort, the physical world will continue to decompose and eventually die until Jesus returns, bringing with him the new heavens and the new earth. Understanding our temporary status in our temporary world reminds us that we should make our mark on this earth with our best efforts, but only as we patiently wait for the next world.

Once I grasped the fact that all my efforts to create beauty and comfort and offer hospitality toward my family and others would have to be repeated many times gave me the insight into the eternal that I had been missing. I remember falsely believing that I was wasting my efforts by cleaning house, washing dishes, doing laundry, and making breakfast, lunch, and dinner every day, year in and year out. I felt as though I was on the repeat cycle of my washing machine and that it would never stop! But then I realized I had to rethink my perspective, and so I did. Living in our sin-ridden, broken world means I have to labor every day for the rest of my life to intentionally create and recreate beauty for those I loved. But isn't this exactly why we serve day in and day out? To create beauty in this space so others might see it and observe the kindness of the Lord through us.

Although it admittedly took me awhile to fully grasp the positive aspect of the author's statement about everything on earth being temporary, once I did I was refueled and reenergized to start serving with renewed determination. No longer did I go about my many daily household tasks with a grimace and inner scorn. Instead, I realized that it is a gift and a privilege to have the opportunity to serve those I love in these daily tasks, and I found joy in the serving (even though some of my efforts didn't last long). My earlier frustration came with attempting to make things right and then make them last forever.

Because we sometimes lose our focus on the eternal, we occasionally give in to the sentiment, "Is this even worth the effort?" We forget that we are sojourners passing through this dry and dusty land. We want to give up when we mistakenly make this earth our permanent home when heaven is our real and eternal home. We spend our efforts trying to make this place better, and then sin's power reminds us that no matter how hard we labor, the truth is that everything on earth is temporary. Yes, at times, that temporal truth stings, but only in the now. Jesus wants us to accept the fact that while we may experience many "repeat cycle" days, in the next life there will be no death or destruction. Just life and glorious life eternal.

## Take-away Action Thought

When I start to feel as though all my hard work and efforts must be continually redone, I will remember that all service, when done for the Lord and others, does last. True, my efforts may not be visible or endure for long from a physical standpoint, but I can find joy in the service, knowing that I am honoring God.

## My Heart's Cry to You, O Lord

Father, there are days when I feel as though everything I do is futile and all my labors seem wasted. I really do struggle with having to repeat my tasks, day in and day out. How I would love for them to last, once and for all. But I recognize that the sinful broken world we now live in is temporary. Sin's curse changed everything. Help me to stay focused on the responsibilities you have set before me today and obey you by joyfully serving others. Remind me that this earth is temporary and that one day soon, you will welcome me to my eternal home. Amen.

## Faith Steps

1. Make a list of the tasks and responsibilities you find yourself grumbling about inwardly. Then ask the Lord to give you a fresh and eternal perspective on the value of serving in the here and now.

2. When you feel discouraged by the seemingly endless list of tasks to be done (over and over again), remind yourself that even the smallest act of love is one of

reverence for God. Turn on worship music as you labor to keep your mind focused on the God who is worthy of all my praise, all the time.

3. Contact several friends and ask them to help you create a monthly plan to create beauty in a shut-in's life. Find creative ways to introduce beauty into their small world.

## Chapter 26

### *Losing All You Have Until All You Have Is Jesus*

He guides me along the right paths
for his name's sake.
Even though I walk
through the darkest valley,
I will fear no evil,
for you are with me.

Psalm 23:3–4

*In time of trouble, say, "First, he brought me here. It is by his will I am in this strait place; in that I will rest." Next, "He will keep me here in his love, and give me grace in this trial to behave as his child." Then say, "He will make the trial a blessing, teaching me lessons he intends me to learn, and working in me the grace he means to bestow. And last, say "In his good time he can bring me out again. How and when, he knows." Therefore, say, "I am here (1) by God's appointment, (2) in his keeping, (3) under his training, (4) for his time."*

*Linda Dillow*

*T*hrough her tears, my good friend told me that her fifty-seven-year-old sister had been officially diagnosed with Alzheimer's. No wonder she was crying. For the past five years, my friend and her family had noticed their sister slipping mentally. Part of the grief comes because fifty-seven is young for an official onset of Alzheimer's, although it's tough even when they're seventy-seven. As we talked about her sister's failing mental abilities and how difficult this disease would become as it grew more severe for her sister and her brother-in-law as caregiver, we lamented on the hardships of aging in general.

Our conversation reminded me of a statement I heard a while ago, "Aging will take it all away and it will take our all . . . until all we have is Jesus. But Jesus is all we need." Wow. Isn't this the truth? Aging will strip away our independence because, eventually, even the most stalwart among us will finally lose the independence we frequently take for granted. As we grow older, we face diminishing mental acuity and sharpness, increasing physical illnesses/diseases, reduction of strength, relationship losses due to death or distance, and energy for daily tasks we can no longer perform safely—driving, exercising, cooking, cleaning, yard work, bathing. The losses are innumerable.

So how do we turn the tables on the losses of aging and make them into offerings we can live with as we press more into the loving arms of Christ? First, I believe each of has to believe the power of this promise: "He guides me along the right paths for his name's sake. Even though I walk through the darkest valley, I will fear no evil, for you are with me." We have to believe that God will lead us where he wants us to go. God will walk beside us into even the darkest valley. And because God is with us, we need not fear anything, including the losses and limitations of old age.

We can only accept these losses as we age can when we place the full weight of our confidence in God to be our all in all. It is true: "Aging will take it all away and it will take our all . . . until all we have is Jesus. But Jesus is all we need."

As I contemplate the fact that I cannot avoid the ravages of aging and time that will eventually override all of my best intentions and healthy habits, I find great comfort in studying how others have dealt with the losses they have faced as they aged. There are three camps from which we can draw inspiration and comfort.

First, we can search the Scriptures and study the heroes of the faith who individually and corporately faced their own losses with a robust faith and their example (and their testimony) of God's faithful goodness will strengthen us for our own journeys.

Second, we can look at history to those individuals who carved out a resilient life despite their sufferings and ordeals. We can study the lives of missionaries who faced death and danger at every turn, even into their twilight years.

Third, we can find encouragement locally. Look around at those folks you know well from your church body, your family, your friends, your colleagues, your neighborhood. Get to know their stories, and invest yourself into their lives so you can glean wisdom from their lives.

"Aging will take it all away and it will take our all . . . until all we have is Jesus. But Jesus is all we need." Yes, aging will eventually take our all; but when we are certain that Jesus is all we need, we can face today (and all our tomorrows) with confidence, peace, and hope with an eternal focus. So, today, find a mentor to inspire you. Engage with your peers for encouragement and support. Give back to a younger person, teaching them all they need to know. Jesus is all we need.

## Take-away Action Thought

When I begin to feel sorry for myself and become discouraged because aging is stripping away my strength and independence, I will remind myself that Jesus is with me and he is all I need.

## My Heart's Cry to You, O Lord

Father, the older I grow, the more keenly aware I am of the limitations that aging places on me physically and on how I live my life. I never want to live in self-pity or give up because I cannot do what I once did. Help me to stay focused on the powerful truth that you lay out my life and you walk with me every day. I need not worry about tomorrow. You have promised to be with me even in the darkest valley, even until my death. Please help me to learn from godly individuals who are older than myself and glean important truths from their example. Help me to willingly surrender my all to you and entrust everything into your faithful care and keeping. Amen.

## Faith Steps

1. When you start to feel self-pity because you are limited by what you can do as you age, search out the Scriptures for the heroes of the faith who were severely challenged and persecuted but who prevailed. Write down the character qualities they exhibited and ask the Lord to begin building those same strengths into you.

129

2. Research missionaries who traveled to the far reaches of the world and faced numerous dangers, trials, and even death for their faith. Spend time reading their biographies and their autobiographies.

3. Contact several godly friends and ask them to help you create a small group where you can jointly invest in, minister to, and mentor younger women.

# Chapter 27

## Help! Help! Help!
## Thank You! Thank You! Thank You!

He gives strength to the weary
and increases the power of the weak.
Even youths grow tired and weary,
and young men stumble and fall;
but those who hope in the LORD
will renew their strength.
They will soar on wings like eagles;
they will run and not grow weary,
they will walk and not be faint.

Isaiah 40:29–31

*There are two kinds of people: the grateful and the
ungrateful. It's the difference between squandering
life and sharing life, between being blinded to glory
and "To God Be the Glory," between assured bitterness
and "Blessed Assurance." It's a difference you can see.*

*Nancy Leigh DeMoss*

*A* much younger, far more energetic me used to pray daily for the stamina to fulfill my role as a mother to four children, ages one through six. A much older, far less energetic me now prays for the stamina to fulfill my role as a grandmother to five grandchildren, ages five months through eight years! In both scenarios, I've done my share of crying out to God for the strength to love these children and grandchildren well. Often my prayers sound like "Help! Help! Help!" followed by "Thank you! Thank you! Thank you!" I've found that both respective cries of the heart are great places to be.

I know I'm not alone in recognizing that I'm alternately crying for help and subsequently giving thanks for help received from God. Just yesterday, I received an e-mail from a friend who will be caring for her four elementary-age grandsons for six days straight. Almost simultaneously, another friend texted, saying she was going to be babysitting her twin four-year-old granddaughters for, you guessed it, six days straight. We went back and forth e-mailing and texting about how grateful we each are to have (1) grandchildren to love, (2) time to invest in their young lives, and (3) Jesus' grace and strength to help us survive those simultaneously wonderful and exhausting grandparenting stints. Because, let's be honest, when we were younger we were thrilled when our children went down for their daily nap. Now, as older women, there are days when all we really want (and need) is to take a nap ourselves!

Which brings me to the ageless principle that no matter how old or young we may be, our universal need is to realize and remember that in our own strength we are not enough. We need Jesus, and he is enough. Young, middle-aged, or older, each of us must accept the reality of our neediness and remember that God is the provider of all we need.

As a younger mom, I often felt bone weary, but I pressed on because my children needed me. As an older woman, I still feel bone weary, but now I press on because my children and grandchildren need me. Once again, I find myself praying "Help! Help! Help!" followed by "Thank you! Thank you! Thank you!" As each year passes, I remind myself that I was just as needy in my twenties, thirties, and forties as I am in my fifties, sixties, and seventies. Asking for help and saying thank you never go out of style.

Today, I may not feel as though I have the stamina to fulfill the responsibilities that lay before me. What I do have, however, is the choice to initiate a dialogue between God and myself about how I feel. When I'm at my lowest ebb, I need to draw all the nearer to the Lord and open up the lines of communication by asking for his help. What more direct prayer is there than "Help! Help! Help!" followed by "Thank you! Thank you! Thank you!"

More often than not, it's my attitude that needs adjusting, not the circumstances. I need to prayerfully review what's ahead of me, make changes as warranted, and focus on giving thanks as a high priority. We frequently get bogged down in the hardships of life, because our perspectives are out of sync with what God's word teaches us. When I feel weak and needy, my confidence cannot be found by mustering up the necessary strength. Rather, my confidence must be in God's supernatural provision to supply my every need (Phil. 4:19). Hence, our prayers for help followed by thanksgiving make all the sense in the world.

When I was younger, I didn't have the option of not pressing through to serve my family. As an older woman, I often do have the option. But God wants me to continue to lean in hard to find my strength in him to fulfill whatever role he places me in at this season of life by serving those people he wants me to impact with his love. I want to end my life knowing my "Blessed Assurance" was helping me, strengthening me all along with way, so that on that final day, I say, "To God be the Glory!" and "Thank you! Thank you! Thank you!"

### Take-away Action Thought

When I begin to feel overwhelmed by my many responsibilities because I don't feel strong enough, I will take the time to pray "Help! Help! Help!" followed by "Thank you! Thank you! Thank you!"

### My Heart's Cry to You, O Lord

Father, I am struggling between being excited about the tasks that lay in front of me this week and feeling overwhelmed by how much I need to accomplish. The older I get, the more hesitant I sometimes feel about committing to opportunities to serve that I believe will stretch my reserves. Help me to be prayerful about saying yes; but once I do, help me to place my full confidence in you to supply the strength I need to serve well. I want to share my life with others by serving them. It's just that I do not have the stamina I once had. My strength must come from you. Amen.

### Faith Steps

1. Write out the above passage from Isaiah 40 and meditate on its truth each day. When you start to feel weary, pray for the stamina to get through this day.

2. At the end of the week, review the past seven days and write down specific ways the Lord helped you fulfill my responsibilities. Make note of how he supernaturally supplied all that you needed to serve well.

3. If any of your friends is actively serving but struggling to do so, offer to assist her through practical means and through prayer.

# Chapter 28

## The Golden Rule of Prayer

Let us then approach God's throne of grace with
confidence, so that we may receive mercy and
find grace to help us in our time of need.

Hebrews 4:16

*It isn't the length of time I spend in my quiet time, though I
usually take an hour, but there is a carry-over of the activity
of prayer, the attitude of prayer, that marks the rest of the day.*

*Stephen Olford*

Our senior pastor taught a message from Matthew 7 recently, and it struck me how the attitude of our hearts toward others affects how we pray in general (and how we intercede on others' behalf). In this passage, Jesus is warning people to remove the huge plank from their own eye before removing the miniscule speck in another's. The point being that if we approach the throne of grace with a judgmental heart toward others, we are not in a fit state to pray with confidence for them (or ourselves).

Our pastor suggested that we test ourselves by asking God one specific, telling question that can determine the state of our hearts in preparedness for rightly approaching the throne of grace: Ask God to reveal any "planks" you are missing in your own heart, before you go into prayer interceding for God to remove the "speck" you are judging in another. Beseech the Lord for personal revelation so you can understand why you feel compelled to judge someone. Is it a matter of clear biblical sin on their part? Or is it mere personal preference to which you are objecting?

In Matthew 7, Jesus provides believers with the proper sequence for handling relationships with others (inside and outside of the faith). First, we are to remove the plank in our own eye before we even consider going to a fellow believer (or praying for them) with the goal of their personal betterment and restoration in mind. We cannot offer up effective prayers for others, if in our hearts we are privately condemning them. Just as Jesus commands us to live by the Golden Rule found in Matthew 7:12—"In everything, do to others what you would have them do to you, for this sums up the Law and the Prophets"—so must we also pray by the Golden Rule.

One aspect of learning to pray rightly is to understand that we always view others (what they think, say, and do) through our own personal filter. If I am the child from an abusive home, I will view abuse in all its forms as especially painful because I have personally lived through the horrors of it myself. If I am the child of a single mom or dad, I will view separation and divorce through the lens of my own personal history. While it is sometimes helpful to call upon our pasts so that we can sympathize and empathize with the trials of others, we forget that we can fall into the judgment trap without being aware of it.

Again, as we look around at the lives of those nearest us and we feel tempted to cast judgment, we should first ask the Lord to reveal our true heart motives, remembering that almost unconsciously we view others through a certain filter. With fresh eyes to see rightly and our hearts cleansed of any sinful motives, we can then approach the throne of grace with confidence. Yes, we must learn to live by the Golden Rule and pray by the Golden Rule. A final personal check is to ask yourself how the world would be different if your prayers were answered!

### Take-away Action Thought

When I feel tempted to judge another person, I will ask the Lord to reveal any impure heart motives I may be harboring. If I am wrongly judging someone, I will confess my sin and offer up a prayer for restoration for the person by praying according to the Golden Rule.

### My Heart's Cry to You, O Lord

Father, help me to be discerning when I pray for others so that I am not unconsciously critical and judgmental in my heart. I know that I have certain areas from my past that remain tender in my heart, and I might unknowingly judge others because of my history. Give me a sensitive spirit toward my own heart intentions, so that when I come before the throne of grace, I can sincerely pray for restoration and healing for others. Let me always purpose to live by the Golden Rule and pray by the Golden Rule of love. My heart's desire is to offer up intercession that helps make this world a better place by changing hearts, one at a time. Amen.

## Faith Steps

1. Spend some quiet time with the Lord each day this week, asking him to reveal any impure heart motives you may have toward others by wrongly judging them. If God reveals any sin on your part, confess it and then start praying for restoration and reconciliation.

2. Every day this week, commit to praying for five specific individuals you know are struggling, remembering to pray in accordance with the Golden Rule.

3. Ask several family members or friends who know you well to share with you any wrong heart attitudes they may have noticed in you toward others. Then invite them to keep you accountable in the future as God brings the issue to mind.

# Chapter 29

## *Bitter and Sweet Make One Flavor*

The LORD is my shepherd, I lack nothing.

Psalm 23:1

*Let us go out with the patient power of knowing that the
God of Israel will go before us. Our yesterdays hold broken
and irreversible things for us. It is true that we have lost
opportunities that will never return, but God can transform
this destructive anxiety into a constructive thoughtfulness
for the future. Let the past rest, but let it rest in the sweet
embrace of Christ. Leave the broken, irreversible past in His
hands, and step out into the invincible future with Him.*

*Oswald Chambers*

*I*n life, there are more than a few major events that I call
the "great magnifiers." First, there are the holidays—
Thanksgiving, Christmas, and Easter. Then there is a
litany of other major events. Births and deaths. Marriages and
divorces. High school and college graduations. Vocational beginnings and endings. Rental or home ownership. Each of these
big life events tends to influence subsequent days, weeks, and
months long after the "event" has happened. And I've found

that with each major life event come the inevitable bitter/sweet repercussions we tend to mull over long afterward in our minds.

After this significant event, we sometimes start second-guessing ourselves. Should I have made a different choice? Could I have said something to alter what happened? Could I have predicted the outcome and avoided it? Depending on your personality, you may not be one of those who looks back or wishes you had said or done something differently. But for the majority of individuals, I believe we spend considerable amounts of time and energy reviewing our major life events by internally wondering how they may have played out differently.

Now, to be clear, reviewing decisions and life happenings can be a positive habit if we do it for the right reason. Are we looking back to figure out what went wrong? Are we rehearsing different outcomes so that we won't make the same mistake in the future? Do we prayerfully spend time remembering painful interactions so we will avoid a disastrous repeat in the coming days and months? Or are we paralyzed by our failure, our missteps, our lack of judgment? Are we unable to enter into a new day confident that because we belong to God he is everything we need?

The biblical truth from Psalm 23 is simple: "The LORD is my shepherd, I lack nothing." Certainly, our lives are a combination of the bitter and sweet, and sometimes it's hard to know the difference between the two as they're so closely entangled.

If you think of your failings as the "bitter" and your successes as the "sweet," then together they make one flavor: bittersweet. This is what makes up the stuff of living in a broken world groaning for redemption. Bitter. Sweet. Bittersweet. You cannot have one without the other.

141

From this day forward, purpose to look in your rearview mirror only when you want to learn from your mistakes. Don't go there to endlessly (and ineffectively) recite your sins, failings, and mistakes over and over again. As Oswald Chambers says, "Let the past rest, but let it rest in the sweet embrace of Christ. Leave the broken, irreversible past in His hands, and step out into the invincible future with Him." Let God do what he does best—redeem. Allow God the opportunity to take what has been broken in your life, whether this is a person, place, or thing, and redeem each one for his glory.

Believe that the Lord is your shepherd and that you lack nothing. Trust his promise to supply your every need to make a new and better start today. You may have a lifetime of bitter memories threatening to swallow you whole, but God is there to tell you that even your bitterest season of suffering has redemptive elements of sweetness hidden there. Ask him to reveal the sweet bit to you today, and remember that bitter and sweet combine to make bittersweet. You cannot have one without the other.

## Take-away Action Thought

When I start to feel paralyzed by my past mistakes, I will recall the promise of Psalm 23:1, "The LORD is my shepherd, I lack nothing." I will ask God to show me how he is working to redeem the bitter and how the sweet can emerge from this pain.

## My Heart's Cry to You, O Lord

Father, help me to accept the truth that this life is filled with both the bitter and the sweet. My past sometimes threatens to overtake my joy for today; and I start to reminisce about old mistakes and failings, only to become paralyzed to try again. Give me the wisdom to look back only as a learning moment so that I can do better in the coming days. I need your divine wisdom and insight to help guide me now and always. I want to honor you by trusting in your supernatural ability to redeem the bitter in my life and transform it into the sweet victories I know you desire for me to experience. Amen.

## Faith Steps

1. This week, memorize Psalm 23:1 and carry the verse with you to review whenever you sit down for a meal. Silently thank the Lord for his faithful and constant work in your life as he transforms you into the likeness of Jesus.

2. Write down any major life events that continue to cause you emotional distress whenever you think about them. Then search through Scripture and locate verses that stand out to you to help you stay strong and help you overcome your past mistakes.

3. This week, invite several good friends to pray with you as you work to view your past errors as redeemable. Share with them how you desire to learn from the bitter and locate the sweet among the past.

 *Chapter 30*

*Leaving a Legacy That Outlasts You*

"Even now my witness is in heaven;
my advocate is on high.
My intercessor is my friend
as my eyes pour out tears to God;
on behalf of a man he pleads with God
as one pleads for a friend."

Job 16:19–21

*Whatever your life situation at this very moment, EVEN
NOW, you have a Witness, an Advocate, an Intercessor,
and a Friend in heaven, making the case before the
Father. That Friend is Jesus Himself, the Son of God
and Creator of all. Whatever your circumstance, doctor's
prognosis, level of pain, bank balance, or earthly
trouble, you have a mighty Witness in heaven who is
completely tuned in to your situation and prays for you.*

*Joni Eareckson Tada and Larry Libby*

hile sitting at a funeral, I noted that the conversation was all about legacies and how we should leave create a life that outlives us. Over the past several months, a half-dozen unexpected deaths have given me cause to think about life and death and legacies. In that order. Each of those within our circle of friends, family, and church died leaving a powerful legacy of faith behind them. As I read their respective obituaries, a common theme struck me. Every one of these Christ followers was active in their local church body where they faithfully served year after year, using the unique gifts and talents God had given them. I also recognized that each of these Christians, apart from their mutual faith in Jesus, had little in common with one another. The tie that bound them together was faith and service and leaving a legacy.

I knew three of those who recently died rather well, and I can attest that they lived out their entire adult lives in the service of Jesus. One woman was a missionary who served in Africa for over twenty years before relocating back to the United States, serving out the remainder of her life as a pastor's wife. The second woman served in her local church, leading dynamic women's studies and was active in Word of Life ministries. The gentleman I knew was a handyman of all trades and used his extensive carpentry skills to build and then maintain church buildings around the city. Life. Death. Legacy. Times three.

Although we applaud their lives (and rightly so), I believe we need to extend our thanksgiving for their faithful service by the way they ended their lives. When fatal illnesses at last triumphed over their physical bodies, these devoted followers of Christ were ushered from earth to heaven. In the weeks leading up to their respective final moments, these faithful servants continued to serve the Lord, not in deeds but through the witness of their lips. They spoke of Jesus as their witness, advocate, intercessor, and friend. They knew he was praying for them at the throne of the Father. They knew it, and we knew it too.

Each of us chooses how we live. We decide whether or not to put to best use the gifts and talents given us by God for our good and his glory. Moment by moment, we are the ones who offer ourselves in service to God and to others. Yes, we can choose to live lives that honor God with the strength he provides; but what we sometimes fail to recognize is that in the same way that we choose to live well, we can also choose to die well. We can honor God with the words we speak and exhibit childlike trust as we cling to this hope during our last hours. Since we know that Jesus is always sitting at the right hand of God the Father interceding on our behalf, we can be confident that he is also advocating for us as our friend until we breathe our final breath.

Knowing that nothing—neither life nor death—will separate us from the love of God, should we not then be as determined, eager even, to make our death one that will rouse the doubting heart to belief in Jesus? We need to consider that the way we choose to say goodbye to this world, as we look upward in faith and hope toward the next one, impacts those we leave behind. What a legacy we can have when we ourselves are fully convinced that Jesus is our witness, advocate, intercessor, and friend.

## Take-away Action Thought

When I near the end of my earthly life, I will linger on those verses that speak of Jesus' constant intercession on my behalf at the throne of the Father. I will prayerfully make plans for my own funeral, so that those who knew me and loved me will take part in my homegoing in a way that will gladden their hearts and glorify God.

## My Heart's Cry to You, O Lord

Father, help me to be desirous of leaving a legacy in both my life and my death. In the same way that I choose to live my life in service to you and others, help me to end my days with the same aim. Help me to see the eternal value of leaving this earthly home with a hope-filled eagerness, as I await a holy reunion with Jesus my Savior and my friend. If there are moments when I feel afraid or anxious, I pray that you will calm me. Through your Holy Spirit, remind me of the wonders that await all who are found in Christ. Give me wisdom and understanding, so I can speak words that are full of childlike trust in you. Amen.

## Faith Steps

1. This week, spend time in silence before the Lord and ask him to reveal to you any gifts or talents that you may have been neglecting to use in service to God and others.

2. With your journal in hand, review your thoughts about how you can leave behind a legacy of faith for the next generation. If you think you haven't been mindful of this Christian witness, make changes to that end.

3. Invite several friends over to discuss their thoughts on leaving a legacy during the end of your lives so you can describe what a good death looks like and how you might prepare your hearts and minds for that eventual day.

# Sources for Quotations

1. Edward Welch (online quote).

2. Randy Alcorn, *90 Days of God's Goodness: Daily Reflections That Shine Light on Personal Darkness* (Colorado Springs: Multnomah, 2011), 254.

3. Linda Dillow, *A Deeper Kind of Calm: Steadfast Faith in the Midst of Adversity* (Colorado Springs: NavPress, 2006), 24.

4. Dillow, *A Deeper Kind of Calm*, 54.

5. Paul David Tripp, *Suffering: Gospel Hope When Life Doesn't Make Sense* (Wheaton, IL: Crossway, 2018), 66.

6. Linda Dillow, *Calm My Anxious Heart* (Colorado Springs: NavPress, 2007), 46.

7. Tripp, *Suffering*, 206.

8. Abraham Kuyper (online quote).

9. Josef Tson (online quote).

10. Max Lucado, *Everyday Blessings: 365 Days of Inspirational Thoughts* (Nashville: Thomas Nelson, 2004), 96.

11. Paul David Tripp, *War of Words: Getting to the Heart of Your Communication Struggles* (Phillipsburg: P & R, 2000), 130.

12. Tripp, *Suffering*, 47.

13. Tripp, *War of Words*, 200.

14. Edward T. Welch, *Running Scared: Fear, Worry, and the God of Rest* (Greensboro: New Growth Press, 2007), 97.

15. Scarlet Hiltibidal, *Afraid of All Things: Tornadoes, Cancer, Adoption, and Other Stuff You Need the Gospel For* (Nashville: B&H, 2018), 136–37.

16. David Livingstone (online quote).

17. Dillow, *Calm My Anxious Heart*, 32.

18. Tripp, *Suffering*, 181.

19. Hiltibidal, *Afraid of All Things*, 189–90.

20. Tripp, *Suffering*, 112.

21. Lucado, *Everyday Blessings*, 192.

22. Tim Lane and Paul Tripp, *Relationships: A Mess Worth Making* (Greensboro: New Growth Press, 2006), 93–94.

23. Ken Sande, *The Peacemaker: A Biblical Guide to Resolving Personal Conflict* (Grand Rapids: Baker, 2006), 176.

24. Nancy Leigh DeMoss, *Choosing Gratitude: Your Journey to Joy* (Chicago: Moody, 2009), 156–57.

25. Lucado, *Everyday Blessings*, 347.

26. Dillow, *Calm My Anxious Heart*, 181.

27. DeMoss, *Choosing Gratitude*, 79.

28. Stephen Olford (online quote).

29. Oswald Chambers, *My Utmost for His Highest* (Grand Rapids: Discovery House, 1992), December 31 entry.

30. Joni Eareckson Tada and Larry Libby, *A Spectacle of Glory: God's Light Shining through Me Every Day* (Grand Rapids: Zondervan, 2016), 38.

## Books by Michele Howe from Hendrickson Publishers & Rose Publishing

*Going It Alone: Meeting the Challenges*
*of Being a Single Mom*

*Still Going It Alone: Mothering with Faith and*
*Finesse When the Children Have Grown*

*Burdens Do a Body Good:*
*Meeting Life's Challenges with Strength (and Soul)*
(with Dr. Christopher A. Foetisch)

*Empty Nest, What's Next? Parenting Adult*
*Children Without Losing Your Mind*

*Caring for Your Aging Parents: Lessons*
*in Love, Loss, and Letting Go*

*Preparing, Adjusting, and Loving the Empty Nest*
A companion to *Empty Nest, What's Next?*

*Navigating the Friendship Maze:*
*The Search for Authentic Friendship*

*There's a Reason They Call It GRANDparenting*

*Strength for All Seasons: A Prayer Devotional*

*Joyous Faith: The Key to Aging with Resilience*

*Living Bravely: Super Incredible Faith Devotional*
(for kids ages 6–9)